# Magento 1.8 Development Cookbook

Over 70 recipes to learn Magento development
from scratch

**Bart Delvaux**

**Nurul Ferdous**

BIRMINGHAM - MUMBAI

# Magento 1.8 Development Cookbook

First published: December 2010

Second Edition: February 2014

Production Reference: 1130214

Published by Packt Publishing Ltd.

Livery Place
35 Livery Street
Birmingham B3 2PB, UK.

ISBN 978-1-78216-332-9

www.packtpub.com

Cover Image by Bart Delvaux (info@bartdelvaux.be)

# Credits

**Authors**
Bart Delvaux
Nurul Ferdous

**Reviewers**
Bartosz Górski
Aron Kerr
Tiago Sampaio

**Acquisition Editors**
Nikhil Karkal
Mary Jasmine Nadar
Dilip Venkatesh

**Content Development Editor**
Athira Laji

**Technical Editors**
Arwa Manasawala
Veena Pagare
Manal Pednekar

**Copy Editors**
Roshni Banerjee
Mradula Hegde
Gladson Monteiro
Adithi Shetty

**Project Coordinator**
Shiksha Chaturvedi

**Proofreaders**
Simran Bhogal
Maria Gould

**Indexer**
Rekha Nair

**Production Coordinator**
Adonia Jones

**Cover Work**
Adonia Jones

# About the Author

**Bart Delvaux** is an experienced web developer from Belgium. With a passion for web technologies, he started his career in 2010 after he received his bachelor's degree in Applied Informatics. Magento gave him the first opportunity to establish himself when he was working as a consultant for a leading PHP company in Belgium. When the Magento certifications were released, Bart was one of the first persons who received Magento Certified Developer and Magento Certified Developer Plus. With the principle of quality above quantity, Bart finished a lot of Magento projects going from a standard web shop to complex integrations and module development.

**Nurul Ferdous** is an open source enthusiast and IT specialist from Bangladesh who is currently working for TM Secure Inc. as a LAMP consultant. In fact, he is a soldier turned programmer. He started his career with the Bangladesh Air Force. He has also served in RAB as an intelligence staff where he was nominated for the President's Police medal for his contribution to national security. He is a true passionate programmer. He started his run on software development back in 2004, while he was working in the Bangladesh Air Force.

His primary skills are as a PHP developer. He is a Zend Certified PHP 5 Engineer, and contributes to a number of PHP projects, blogs on PHP-related topics, and presents talks and tutorials related to PHP development and the projects to which he contributes. He also contributes on open source community regularly. He is also a certified professional on TDD and Code Refactoring.

He has served in some top notch software companies both at home and abroad, such as BIPL, Right Brain Solutions Ltd., TM Secure Inc., NameDepot.com Inc., and so on, as a programmer, software engineer, and consultant. He also writes at his personal blog `http://dynamicguy.com` when he is not baking with codes.

The very first person whom I would like to thank who made this happen is Dilip Venkatesh along with Meeta Rajani, Aditi Suvarna, and all Packt Publishing personnel who worked on this book. I am also thankful to my wife, Ferdousy Chowdhury and my kid, Riva. They have helped me a lot during the whole writing process!

# About the Reviewers

**Bartosz Górski** is a Magento Certified Developer Plus and a Magento Certified Frontend Developer working for Creatuity, a Magento Silver Solution Partner. He has been working in the web development and programming field for over six years, and has over three years of experience in developing only for the Magento e-commerce platform.

Bartosz is a big fan of doing things the right way, so he always aims to write as clean and efficient code as possible. He's always happy to give and receive feedback on how a given piece of code can be improved.

When he's not at work, he's probably playing pool somewhere, sitting at home and browsing camera lenses on eBay, and complaining about how little time he has to actually go outside and click some photos himself.

I'd like to thank my wife for her love and support (and for not killing me in some cruel way when I'm spending another evening with Magento instead of spending it with her).

**Tiago Sampaio** began to develop modules and implementations for Magento Commerce in 2010 for a college project. He has now become one of the most famous Magento developers in Brazil.

With four years of experience in Magento platform development, he was the first one to pass the Magento Certified Developer Plus exam. Today, he is a unique developer who has all of the three available Magento certifications. In order of relevance, the certifications owned by Tiago are Magento Front End Developer (June 2013), Magento Certified Developer (December 2012), and Magento Certified Developer Plus (January 2013).

With extensive experience in Magento development, Tiago is specialized in the platform and nowadays works only with Magento developments as a Software Development Team Leader at e-smart, a unique Magento Gold partner in Brazil.

First, I'd like to thank God for giving me the opportunity to change my life by learning about Magento Commerce and making me not give up during the most hard times of my life. I would also like to thank my family and friends for all the support they gave me and for staying by my side all the time giving me strength to always go on with my daily battles. Thanks to Packt Publishing for this great opportunity to participate in this book, which I guess, will be one of the most important books to disseminate experiences and knowledge about Magento Commerce to the whole world.

# www.PacktPub.com

## Support files, eBooks, discount offers and more

You might want to visit www.PacktPub.com for support files and downloads related to your book.

Did you know that Packt offers eBook versions of every book published, with PDF and ePub files available? You can upgrade to the eBook version at www.PacktPub.com and as a print book customer, you are entitled to a discount on the eBook copy. Get in touch with us at service@packtpub.com for more details.

At www.PacktPub.com, you can also read a collection of free technical articles, sign up for a range of free newsletters and receive exclusive discounts and offers on Packt books and eBooks.

http://PacktLib.PacktPub.com

Do you need instant solutions to your IT questions? PacktLib is Packt's online digital book library. Here, you can access, read and search across Packt's entire library of books.

## Why Subscribe?

▶ Fully searchable across every book published by Packt

▶ Copy and paste, print and bookmark content

▶ On demand and accessible via web browser

## Free Access for Packt account holders

If you have an account with Packt at www.PacktPub.com, you can use this to access PacktLib today and view nine entirely free books. Simply use your login credentials for immediate access.

# Table of Contents

# Preface

Magento is one of the most popular e-commerce platforms on the market because it is free, stable, and offers a lot of functionalities. A lot of e-commerce websites are built with Magento. Developing in Magento is not as easy as you would expect. When you want to start with Magento, a good guide that shows you the best practices will be very helpful while learning Magento development, and that is what this book has set out to do.

With *Magento 1.8 Development Cookbook*, we will discover all the topics that will help you become a good Magento developer, and then we start with the basics and end with more advanced topics towards the end of this book. This will be a good guideline that explains every step or action that you have to take to complete the recipes of this book.

We will start this book with the creation of a good development environment using the right tools. We will create a web server where we will put a Magento installation with sample products in it. We will create a custom theme to change the look and feel of the webshop. The focus of this book will be the development part. We will create a custom module that follows the best practices of Magento. We will customize this module with a lot of common features that are used in Magento projects, such as extra controller pages, database integrations, custom shipping methods, and extra backend interfaces. At the end of the book, we will see how we can improve the performance of our Magento installation. Finally, we will see some debugging techniques such as xDebug and create a unit test with PHPUnit.

## What this book covers

*Chapter 1, Getting Started with Magento*, gives you an introduction and shows you how to create a development environment using the right tools, how to install Magento, and how to work with the code in a version control system.

*Chapter 2, Theming*, explains what you can do to customize the look and feel of your shop.

*Chapter 3, Working with Products*, gives you more information about the possibilities of showing the products in your shop and customizing the product pages with a Facebook like button.

*Chapter 4*, *Creating a Module*, describes how to create a basic Magento module, how to extend that module with configurations for a custom page, translations, blocks, and how to rewrite existing classes.

*Chapter 5*, *Database Concepts*, shows you how Magento works with database connections, how the tables are linked to Magento entities, and how the EAV system works. It also shows you how to create a Master/Slave setup.

*Chapter 6*, *Databases and Modules*, teaches you how to extend a Magento module with a database interaction by creating an install script that installs a database table and entity that will interact with this database table.

*Chapter 7*, *Magento Backend*, covers the topics that you should know when integrating your module with the Magento backend, such as adding extra configuration pages, creating overview pages, and extending the admin menu.

*Chapter 8*, *Event Handlers and Cronjobs*, describes how the Event-driven Architecture is implemented in Magento and how you can use this in a module. Later in this chapter, you will learn how to create cronjobs in a module and how to test them.

*Chapter 9*, *Creating a Shipping Module*, shows you how to create a custom module with the configurations required for a new shipping method.

*Chapter 10*, *Creating a Product Slider Widget*, explains how to create a module with a custom widget, how to build the backend interface, and how to provide a good UI in the frontend of that widget.

*Chapter 11*, *Performance Optimization*, describes how to benchmark your site to know the limits and improve its performance using different techniques such as web server optimization and caching systems (APC and Memcached).

*Chapter 12*, *Debugging and Unit Testing*, shows you how to use the PHP debugger xDebug, how to use FirePHP in Magento, and how to create a simple unit test with PHPUnit.

# What you need for this book

- Magento 1.8 source code
- Ubuntu Version 13.10 or higher
- Apache2
- PHP Version 5.3 or higher
- MySQL Server 5
- NetBeans IDE
- phpMyAdmin
- Wiz command-line tool

- Firebug (add-on for Firefox)
- FirePHP (add-on for Firefox)
- xDebug
- PHPUnit
- A standard web browser
- Siege (a benchmarking tool)
- ApacheBench (another benchmarking tool)
- YSlow (add-on for Firefox)
- Git SCM
- jQuery
- carouFredSel (a jQuery library to create a jQuery carousel)

# Who this book is for

If you know something about programming in PHP and want to start with Magento development, this book has something for you. Knowledge of Magento is not required to start with the recipes of this book. Basic knowledge of PHP and web development is required. This book starts with the fundamentals of Magento development and ends with more advanced topics. Even if you know something about Magento development yet you need a good guide, this book has something for you.

# Conventions

In this book, you will find a number of styles of text that distinguish between different kinds of information. Here are some examples of these styles, and an explanation of their meaning.

Code words in text, database table names, folder names, filenames, pathnames, dummy URLs and user inputs are shown as follows: "The `widget.xml` file is used to define widgets in the Magento installation."

A block of code is set as follows:

```
<category_id>
    <label>Category ID</label>
    <type>text</type>
    <required>1</required>
    <sort_order>20</sort_order>
    <visible>1</visible>
</category_id>
```

When we wish to draw your attention to a particular part of a code block, the relevant lines or items are set in bold:

```
<category_id>
    <label>Category ID</label>
    <type>text</type>
    <required>1</required>
    <sort_order>20</sort_order>
    <visible>1</visible>
</category_id>
```

Any command-line input or output is written as follows:

```
sudo apt-get install apache2
```

**New terms** and **important words** are shown in bold. Words that you see on the screen, in menus or dialog boxes, for example, appear in the text like this: "Click on **Finish** and your NetBeans project is ready."

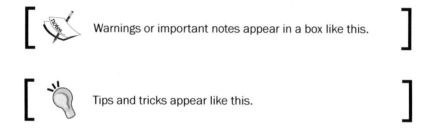

Warnings or important notes appear in a box like this.

Tips and tricks appear like this.

# Reader feedback

Feedback from our readers is always welcome. Let us know what you think about this book—what you liked or may have disliked. Reader feedback is important for us to develop titles that you really get the most out of.

To send us general feedback, simply send an e-mail to feedback@packtpub.com, and mention the book title via the subject of your message.

If there is a topic that you have expertise in and you are interested in either writing or contributing to a book, see our author guide on www.packtpub.com/authors.

# Customer support

Now that you are the proud owner of a Packt book, we have a number of things to help you to get the most from your purchase.

## Downloading the example code

You can download the example code files for all Packt books you have purchased from your account at `http://www.packtpub.com`. If you purchased this book elsewhere, you can visit `http://www.packtpub.com/support` and register to have the files e-mailed directly to you.

## Errata

Although we have taken every care to ensure the accuracy of our content, mistakes do happen. If you find a mistake in one of our books—maybe a mistake in the text or the code—we would be grateful if you would report this to us. By doing so, you can save other readers from frustration and help us improve subsequent versions of this book. If you find any errata, please report them by visiting `http://www.packtpub.com/submit-errata`, selecting your book, clicking on the **errata submission form** link, and entering the details of your errata. Once your errata are verified, your submission will be accepted and the errata will be uploaded on our website, or added to any list of existing errata, under the Errata section of that title. Any existing errata can be viewed by selecting your title from `http://www.packtpub.com/support`.

## Piracy

Piracy of copyright material on the Internet is an ongoing problem across all media. At Packt, we take the protection of our copyright and licenses very seriously. If you come across any illegal copies of our works, in any form, on the Internet, please provide us with the location address or website name immediately so that we can pursue a remedy.

Please contact us at `copyright@packtpub.com` with a link to the suspected pirated material.

We appreciate your help in protecting our authors, and our ability to bring you valuable content.

## Questions

You can contact us at `questions@packtpub.com` if you are having a problem with any aspect of the book, and we will do our best to address it.

# 1
# Getting Started with Magento

In this chapter, we will cover the following topics:

- ▶ Preparing the development environment
- ▶ Installing Magento with sample data
- ▶ Adding version control to the source code
- ▶ Configuring the development tools

## Introduction

You have probably heard of Magento. It is an out-of-the-box e-commerce platform with many features, such as catalog navigation, promotion rules, RSS feeds, product search, product tags, product reviews, tax rules, reports, and order management.

The company behind Magento is Varien. In 2007, they started thinking about an open source e-commerce platform that would be designed for a large number of uses. After one year of developing, the first stable release Magento 1.0 came out in 2008. When Magento became more popular in the later years, eBay showed interest in it and now owns 100 percent of Magento.

If you install Magento and configure it, then you can start selling products online. But when you want a custom theme, extra shipping methods, and other features, you have to extend the software as per the rules of Magento. If you know something about PHP programming, follow the steps described in the recipes, and you can start editing your Magento store.

We will create a development environment where you can start working. We will install sample data so that the shop is not empty and is ready to go. If you are new, you can start here. If you are a pro, you can still start here, because we follow the best practices of Magento development. Let's get started. Good luck!

# Preparing the development environment

We will set up a development environment with Magento. For this, we need to set up a **LAMP** (**Linux, Apache, MySQL, PHP**) environment. In that LAMP environment, we will create a **Fully Qualified Domain Name** (**FQDN**) and a virtual host.

## Getting ready

We have to set up a development server that we will use to run Magento. When we have a Ubuntu desktop environment, we have to install the latest versions of the following software:

- Apache2
- PHP
- MySQL server
- Extra PHP libraries

We can install these software by running the following commands on a CLI interface. These commands are based on a Ubuntu-based Linux distribution. To run the commands on a desktop with Ubuntu OS, launch the **Terminal** program:

- To install the web server Apache2, run the following command:

  ```
  sudo apt-get install apache2
  ```

- To install PHP, run the following command:

  ```
  sudo apt-get install php5
  ```

- To install the MySQl server, run the following command:

  ```
  sudo apt-get install mysql-server
  ```

- To install the required PHP extensions that Magento uses, such as the MySQL bridge, run the following command:

  ```
  sudo apt-get install php5-mysql php5-curl php5-gd php-pear
  ```

## How to do it...

When everything is installed, we will create a virtual host with an FQDN. We want our development environment to be available at `http://magento-dev.local/`. To do this, we have to create a virtual host with this domain name. This domain points to the IP of our previously created web server.

The following steps describe how you can create a virtual host with an FQDN:

1. Create a `magento-dev.local` file in the `/etc/apache2/sites-available/` directory.

2. To create and edit the file, run the following command:

   **`sudo nano /etc/apache2/sites-available/magento-dev.local`**

3. Paste the following content in that file:

   ```
   <VirtualHost *:80>
    # ServerName (domain) and admin email
    ServerAdmin webmaster@magento-dev.local
    ServerName magento-dev.local


    DocumentRoot /var/www/magento-dev.local/public # Folder of the
   site. We have to create this

    # Log file locations
    LogLevel warn
    ErrorLog /var/log/apache2/magento-dev.error.log
    CustomLog /var/log/apache2/magento-dev.access.log combined
   </VirtualHost>
   ```

4. Run the following commands in the terminal to create the www root folder:

   1. To create the site folder (document root), run the following command:

      **`sudo mkdir /var/www/magento-dev.local/public`**

      **`sudo chown -R www-data:www-data /var/www/magento-dev.local/`**

   2. To enable the site, run the following command:

      **`sudo a2ensite magento-dev.local`**

   3. To reload the Apache server, run the following command:

      **`sudo service apache2 reload`**

4. To test the site, we have to add the following line in our host's file (/etc/hosts):

```
127.0.0.1 magento-dev.local
```

This will point the domain magento-dev.local to the IP address 127.0.0.1. This is the IP address of the local web server (localhost), so a request to this URL doesn't go to the Internet but goes to the local web server.

## How it works...

This recipe describes how to install a web server from a CLI interface. If you already have a web server with a specific domain, you can skip this chapter.

The Magento files will be installed in the public directory. When a request is made to the domain, the www-data user will execute the request. So, it is best that all files and folders have the www-data user and group to avoid permission problems.

On a Linux server, every file and folder has three types of permissions. These permissions are **read**, **write**, **and execute** (**rwx**). You can set these permissions in three scopes: for owners, groups, and others. On every file request, Linux decides, based on the permissions, whether a user can read, write, or execute a certain file.

For an HTTP request, the www-data user will be used to execute a request. So, it is important to ensure that the www-data user has enough file permissions to run the application. To change file permissions, you can use the chmod command. To change the owner and group, you can use the chown command.

## There's more...

It is also possible to run Magento and the web server on other operating systems. To run a web server, we need Apache, MySQL, and PHP. It is possible to install these software on a Windows or Mac device.

The variant for Windows operating systems is **WAMP** (**Windows, Apache, MySQL, and PHP**). You can find more information about this variant on the WAMP website at http://www.wampserver.com.

For Mac OS, the alternative is MAMP. More information on MAMP is available at http://www.mamp.info.

A cross-platform web server is XAMP. You can download the installer for Linux, Windows, or Mac from their website at http://www.apachefriends.org/en/xampp.html.

# Installing Magento with sample data

When you install Magento, you can start with an empty database or a database with some sample products and configurations. For our development environment, the best approach is to start with the sample data because we can start using Magento directly after installation.

For a new webshop, it is recommended to start with an empty database and do the configuration yourself. To install Magento, we need the following data:

- The Magento code
- The sample data

## Getting ready

You can download Magento and the sample data from Magento's website (http://www. magentocommerce.com/download). Download the latest **Full release** and the **Sample data**. The recipes of this book are based on the Magento Version 1.8.1.0. For the sample data, you can use the 1.6.1.0 Version.

## How to do it...

The following steps show you how to install a clean Magento webshop with sample data:

1. Extract the code in the appropriate folder of our web server. In our case, this is /var/ www/magento-dev.local/public. Take a look at the folder structure by running the ls -la command in the site's root folder. We have to take care that the hidden files are included in the folder:

```
ls -la
drwxrwxr-x .
drwxrwxr-x ..
-rwxrw-r-- .htaccess
-rw-rw-r-- .htaccess.sample
-rw-rw-r-- api.php
drwxrwxr-x app
-rw-rw-r-- cron.php
-rw-rw-r-- cron.sh
drwxrwxr-x downloader
drwxrwxr-x errors
-rw-rw-r-- favicon.ico
-rw-rw-r-- get.php
-rw-rw-r-- .htaccess
```

```
-rw-rw-r--  .htaccess.sample
drwxrwxr-x  includes
-rw-rw-r--  index.php
-rw-rw-r--  index.php.sample
-rw-rw-r--  install.php
drwxrwxr-x  js
drwxrwxr-x  lib
-rw-rw-r--  LICENSE_AFL.txt
-rw-rw-r--  LICENSE.html
-rw-rw-r--  LICENSE.txt
-rw-rw-r--  mage
drwxrwxr-x  media
-rw-rw-r--  php.ini.sample
drwxrwxr-x  pkginfo
-rw-rw-r--  RELEASE_NOTES.txt
drwxrwxr-x  shell
drwxrwxr-x  skin
drwxrwxr-x  var
```

In Linux, hidden files or folders start wit a dot (.), such as the `.htaccess` file. The `-a` option of the `ls` command that we used shows all the files and folders, including the hidden ones. It is important to see that the `.htaccess` file is in the directory because this file contains the configuration for URL rewrites and other server configurations.

2.  When you extract the sample data archive, you see a media folder and a SQL file. The SQL file contains the database, the media folder, and the images. To install the media folder, merge this folder with the site's root media folder.

It is important to install the sample data before running the Magento install wizard. If Magento doesn't find the sample data in the database, the wizard continues with an empty database without the sample data.

3.  To install the database, you have to run the following commands:

    1.  To create the database, run the following commands:

        ```
        mysql -u root -p
        create database magento_dev;
        exit;
        ```

    2.  To import the SQL file, run the following commands:

        ```
        mysql -u <<username>> -p magento_dev <
        "path_to_sample_data.sql"
        ```

To avoid permission problems, ensure that all files and folders have the right permissions. For security reasons, it is recommended that all files have just enough permissions so that only the right users can access the right files. When you give all the rights (777), you don't have permission problems; but, every user on the server can read, write, and execute every file of your application.

4. The next step is to run the Magento installation wizard. Go to the site's URL and the installer will be displayed as shown in the following screenshot:

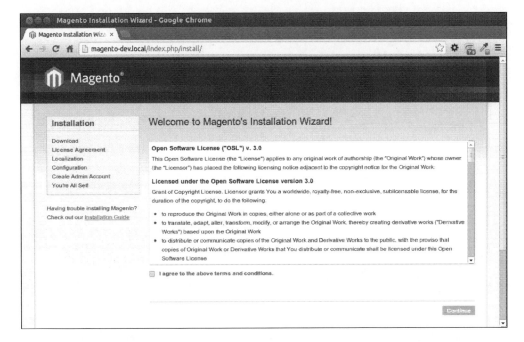

5. Continue with the installation process by accepting the terms and conditions.

6. On the next screen, choose the correct language, locale, and currency for your store.

7. On the **Configuration** page, fill the form with the right data:

   - **Database Type**: Enter `MySQL` in this field.
   - **Host**: Enter `localhost` in this field.
   - **Database Name**: Enter `magento_dev` (your Magento database name) in this field.
   - **User Name**: Enter `root` (your Magento database username) in this field.
   - **User Password**: Enter `root` (your database user password) in this field. It is possible to leave this empty.

- ❑ **Tables Prefix**: Leave this field empty (if filled, all tables will have the prefix that is entered here).
- ❑ **Base URL**: Enter `http://magento-dev.local/` (the URL of your webshop) in this field.
- ❑ **Admin Path**: Enter `admin` (the path to the backend) in this field.
- ❑ **Enable Charts**: This check box must be checked.
- ❑ **Skip Base URL Validation Before the Next Step**: This check box must be unchecked (if checked, the wizard will check for a valid URL when processing this form).
- ❑ **Use Web Server (Apache) Rewrites**: This check box must be unchecked.
- ❑ **Use Secure URLs (SSL)**: This check box must be unchecked.

8. Submit the form and continue to the next step. In this step, you can configure the admin account. Fill in the right data and remember the login and password, because this is required to manage the store. Leave the encryption key empty.

9. After submitting this form, the installation wizard terminates. The setup is complete. You can now visit your store and enter the backend with the username that you have created in the installation wizard.

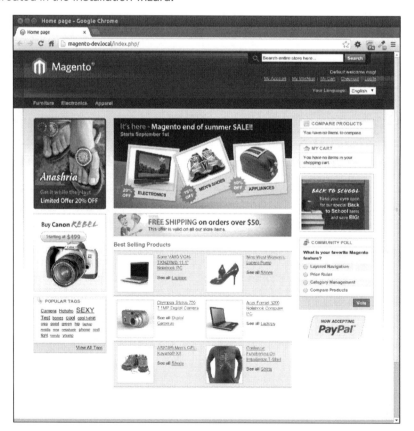

## How it works...

We just created a fully functional Magento store. Technically, you can start selling products.

We have started with the sample data. The SQL file that we inserted in the database contains all the data for the sample webshop. When you want to create an empty shop, you can start with an empty database.

When installing a new shop, always follow the installer. The installer creates the `app/etc/local.xml` file and installs the values that you have set in the installer. These values are currency, timezone, backend user, and so on. The installer will show up when there is no `local.xml` file in the `app/etc/` folder. In all other cases, the webshop will show up.

With a complete `local.xml` file in the `app/etc` folder, you can install Magento. However, this is not recommended because you don't have a backend user and the other configurations.

# Adding version control to the source code

With version control, you can manage the changes that are made in the computer files. When you add this to a programming code, you can track all the changes you have made to the code from the time you initialized it. There are some very popular version control systems on the market, such as Subversion (SVN), Mercurial SCM, CVS, and Git SCM.

In this recipe, we will use Git SCM to add version control to our previously created Magento code. We will initialize an empty repository. After that, we will do several commits to add all the Magento code to the repository.

## Getting ready

Go to your command line, and install Git on your local server by running the following command in the terminal:

```
sudo apt-get install git
```

## How to do it...

The following steps show you how you can add the Magento code to the version control system Git:

1.  We have to initialize the Git repository. To do this, navigate to the source folder and enter the following command:

    ```
    git init
    ```

2. Run the following command and you will see that all the files are marked as untracked:

```
git status
```

In the next steps, we will add the other folders to the repository.

3. Add the `app/` folder to the repository by running the following command:

```
git add app/
```

This will add all the files in the `app/` directory. When you run the `git status` command, you will see a list of all the files.

4. Run the following command to remove the `local.xml` file from the repository but not from the drive:

```
git rm --cached app/etc/local.xml
```

5. Run the following command to create the first commit:

```
git commit -m "add app folder"
```

6. Run the following command to track the file's status:

```
git status
```

7. Create a `.gitignore` file in the root, and add the following content in it:

```
app/etc/local.xml
```

8. Run the `git status` command again, and you will see that `local.xml` is ignored.

9. Commit the `.gitignore` file by running the following command:

```
git commit .gitignore -m "add gitignore file"
```

10. Add the other application files and folders to the repository by running the command `git add <folder or filename>`. Run this command for the following folders:

- ❏ `downloader` (for installing plugins)
- ❏ `errors` (configuration about error handling)
- ❏ `js` (the JS library folder)
- ❏ `lib` (contains PHP libraries)
- ❏ `pkginfo` (information about upgrades)
- ❏ `shell/` (contains PHP CLI scripts)
- ❏ `skin/` (the CSS and images folder)
- ❏ `api.php`
- ❏ `cron.php`
- ❏ `cron.sh`

- ❏ `favicon.ico`
- ❏ `get.php`
- ❏ `index.php`
- ❏ `index.php.sample`
- ❏ `install.php`
- ❏ `LICENCE_AFL.txt`
- ❏ `LICENCE.html`
- ❏ `LICENCE.txt`
- ❏ `mage`
- ❏ `php.ini.sample`
- ❏ `RELEASE_NOTES.txt`

11. Run a new `git commit` command:

    ```
    git commit -m "add additional files"
    ```

12. Ignore the other nonstatic Magento files and folders. Add the following content in the `.gitignore` file:

    `/app/etc/local.xml`

    `/errors/local.xml`

    ```
    /media/css/
    /media/dhl
    /media/downloadable
    /media/import/
    /media/js/
    /media/catalog/
    /media/customer
    /media/upload/
    /media/wysiwyg/
    /media/captcha/
    /media/tmp/
    /media/xmlconnect
    ```

    ```
    /var/import/
    /var/export/
    /var/cache/
    /var/log/
    /var/session/
    ```

```
/var/locks/
/var/package
/var/report/
/var/resource_config.json

sitemap.xml
```

13. Add the `media/` and `var/` folders to the repository with the following command:

    **git add media/.htaccess**

    **git add var/.htaccess**

    We only need the `.htaccess` files, the other files are ignored because they are dynamic.

## How it works...

When working with a version control system, you have to keep in mind that another person who clones the project can set up the environment with a database and the code in the Git. That environment has to be the same as the one you have committed.

It is very important that every Magento core file and your customized files are in the Git repository. You don't have to add configuration files, such as `app/etc/local.xml` and `errors/local.xml`, in version control. When running your code on another server, the settings in the configuration files are mostly different from the settings on the server.

Dynamically generated files such as cache files and user images are stored in the `media` and `var` folder, so we don't need the content of these folders.

The only important file in these folders is the `.htaccess` file, which has the configuration to restrict the `var` folder and the `media` folder.

# Configuring the development tools

When you start customizing your Magento store, a good development environment with the following components saves time:

 ▸ A code editor (IDE)

 ▸ A MySQL client (phpMyAdmin or MySQL Workbench)

 ▸ A command-line tool

## Getting ready

NetBeans is an open source IDE that can be used for a lot of programming languages. The PHP support is well maintained and there are a lot of integrations with other systems (Git, SVN, and MySQL).

To install NetBeans, you have to download it from their site at `http://netbeans.org` and run the installer. Make sure that when you download it, you select the PHP version or the full version.

## How to do it...

The following steps show you how to create a NetBeans project with the Magento files as the document root:

1. To create the project, open NetBeans and navigate to **File | New Project**.

2. In the dialog window, click on **PHP Application with Existing Sources** as shown in the following screenshot:

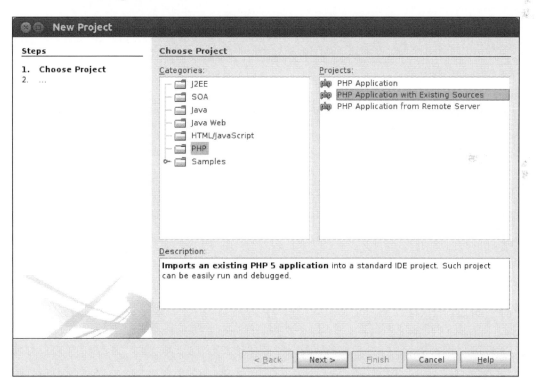

3.  Click on **Next** and configure the following settings:

    ❏ **Source Folder**: This field is set to the location of your Magento code

    ❏ **Project Name**: The NetBeans project name is entered in this field

    ❏ **PHP Version**: This field is set to **PHP 5.3** or higher

    ❏ **Default Encoding**: This field is set to **UTF-8**

    The following screenshot gives the sample values for these settings:

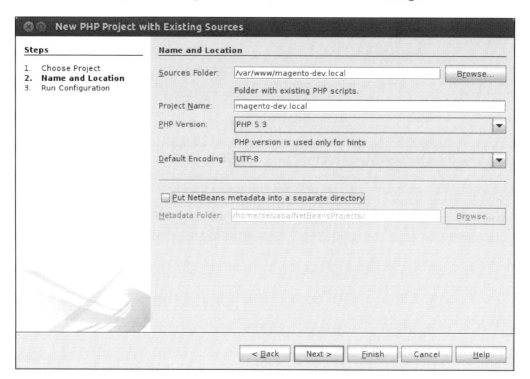

 When you are working with a version control system (SVN, Git, or something else), it is recommended to check the option **Put NetBeans metadata into a separate directory**. If not checked, a .nbproject folder is created in your Magento root, which you will not have in your version control system. Another possibility is to add the .nbproject folder in the .gitignore file.

4.  Click on **Next**.

5. Configure the following settings:

 ❑ **Run as:** In our case, this field is set to a local web server

 ❑ **Project URL**: In this field, enter `http://magento-dev.local`, the URL that we have configured for Magento

 ❑ **Index File**: This field is set to `index.php`

The following screenshot gives the sample values for these settings:

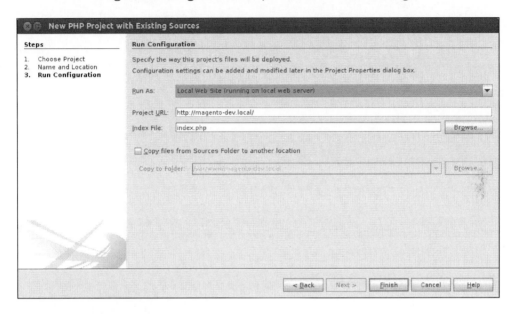

6. Click on **Finish** and your NetBeans project is ready.

## How it works...

When the project is started, you see the document root in the left-hand side column of the window. When you double click on a file, the file will open in the main window. In this window, you can view the file's history, format the code, refactor variable names, and a lot more.

## There's more...

Behind the development environment in the IDE, a database client and a command-line tool are very useful when developing in Magento.

## MySQL client phpMyAdmin

phpMyAdmin is a MySQL client that runs as a web application. It is an easy-to-use tool for direct SQL input in a database.

1. To install phpMyAdmin, open your terminal and run the following command:

   ```
   sudo apt-get install phpmyadmin
   ```

2. Follow the installer's instructions.

3. Edit the `/etc/apache2/apache.conf` file, and add the following code at the end of the file:

   ```
   Include /etc/phpmyadmin/apache.conf
   ```

4. Reload the Apache server with the following command:

   ```
   sudo service apache2 reload
   ```

5. Go to `http://magento-dev.local/phpmyadmin`, and you will see the login screen. You can log in with the credentials of the database user for your Magento database.

## Command-line tool Wiz

Magento has a lot of system tasks that you have to execute in your development process. All these actions could be triggered in the backend. However, because this is a time consuming job, a shell interface can save you a lot of time.

Wiz is a command-line tool that you can download from `https://github.com/classyllama/Wiz`.

Follow the installation instructions on their website. When installed, you have to change the directory of your shell to your Magento root. If you are in the Magento root, all the commands you run are executed for that Magento installation.

The following are some useful commands:

- `wiz admin-resetpass`: This command can be used when you forget your admin password
- `wiz admin-createadmin`: This command creates a new administrative user from scratch
- `wiz cache-clear`: This command clears all cache or specific cache
- `wiz devel-showhints`: This command enables or disables frontend hints
- `wiz module-list`: This command gives a list of all the installed modules
- `wiz sql-cli`: This command opens the MySQL command line

# 2
# Theming

In this chapter, we will cover the following topics:

- ▶ Configuring Magento themes and packages
- ▶ Creating your first theme
- ▶ Adding extra files to your theme
- ▶ Adding jQuery support
- ▶ Changing a page title
- ▶ Working with translations
- ▶ Understanding the theming block system
- ▶ Adding widgets to the layout

## Introduction

When you want to make your sample Magento site ready for use, the first thing most people want to change is the look and feel of the shop. The first impression a visitor has of your site is the look and feel.

In this chapter, we will cover the most important things you can do with a Magento theme. Customizing the standard theme is not so difficult but building a theme from scratch is a lot of work.

## Configuring Magento themes and packages

Magento works with multiple themes. You can configure more themes in the same store. A common case is that you have a theme of your shop and some inherited themes based on the shop theme.

## Getting ready

Log in to the backend and go to the theme configuration section that you can find at **System | Configuration | Design**.

## How to do it...

The following instructions describe how to manage the different Magento themes of a webshop:

1. Change the theme field to `modern` and clear the cache. Go to your frontend and your shop will look as follows:

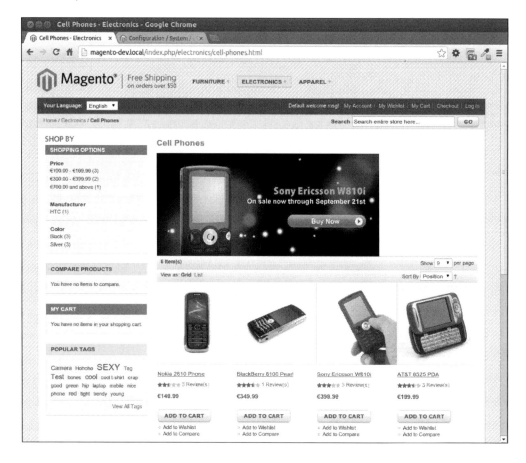

You have now configured the `modern` theme in the `default` package. This theme will extend things from the `default` theme and, in the last case, from the `base/default` theme. This process is called the **theme fallback system**.

2. Make the theme field empty and add the following configuration:

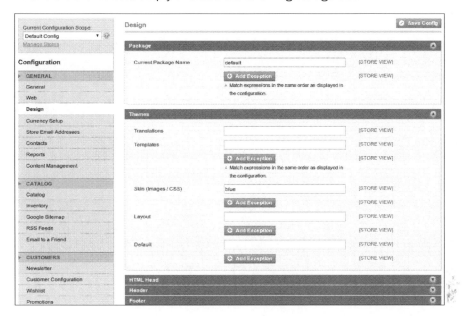

3. Reload the frontend:

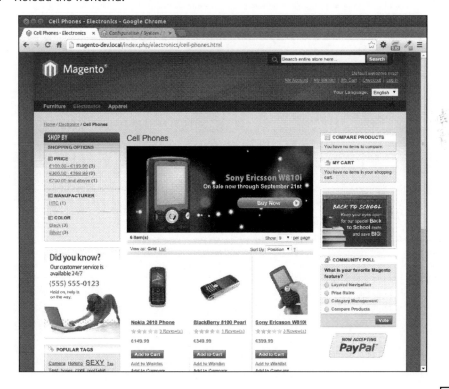

Your shop will look like the `default` theme but with some different CSS styles. We have configured the `default` theme but with another `skin` folder that contains the CSS files.

## How it works...

There are three levels of themes in Magento: the base theme, the package's default theme, and the other themes in the package.

The following diagram shows how the theme fallback system works when you have configured a theme:

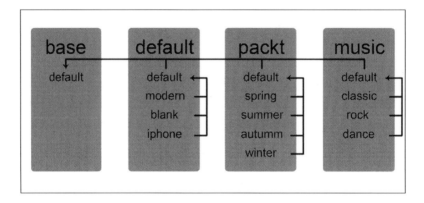

When the `winter` theme is configured, Magento will look at files in the following order:

- ▸ The theme (`packt/winter`)
- ▸ The package's default theme (`packt/default`)
- ▸ The base theme (`base/default`)

It is possible to configure a default theme in the configuration page by navigating to **System | Configuration | Design**. If this is set (for example, `packt/summer`), the fallback system will loop through the themes in the following order:

- ▸ The theme (`packt/winter`)
- ▸ The configured default theme (`packt/summer`)
- ▸ The package's default theme (`packt/default`)
- ▸ The base theme (`base/default`)

The directory where the theme is stored is `app/design/frontend` for the template files (rendering HTML) and `skin/frontend` for the static files (CSS, images, fonts, and so on).

Practically, the default theme of a package will contain the theme of the webshop. The subthemes in that package mostly have the same layout but differ in some small things. For example, a winter theme has a background with snow and the summer theme has a background with a beach. The rest of the theme is exactly the same because this uses the same files of the default theme.

When your theme is not in the default package, nothing happens on the frontend after installing a Magento extension.

The reason could be that the theme files of the module are in the default package. Magento looks only at the configured and base packages. The default package is just like every other package such as `packt` or `music`. When a module has custom theme files, the best practice is to store these files in the base theme to avoid this problem.

You can configure Magento themes on different levels to show up on the frontend. In most cases, the theme settings are configured on the configuration page by navigating to **System | Configuration | Design**.

You can add exceptions on the page by navigating to **System | Design**. On this page, you can configure a theme for a store with a from date and to date.

It is also possible to configure a specific theme for a product, category, or CMS page. You can change the settings on the edit pages of a product, category, or CMS page.

# Creating your first theme

We will create a package with a default theme in it. At a later stage, we can add more themes in this package, which extend the default theme that we will create in this chapter.

## Getting ready

Open your IDE and navigate to the theme folder (`app/design/frontend and skin/frontend/default`).

## How to do it...

The following procedure shows you which actions are required to create a custom theme:

1.  Create the following folders:

    ❑   `app/design/frontend/packt/default`
    ❑   `app/design/frontend/packt/default/layout`

❑ app/design/frontend/packt/default/template

❑ skin/frontend/packt/default

2. Copy the content of the folder skin/frontend/default/blank/ to skin/
   frontend/packt/default. The folder looks as follows:

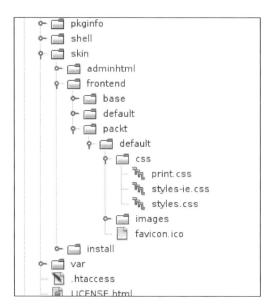

3. Configure the new theme and package in the backend. Navigate to **System |
   Configuration | Design** and configure as follows:

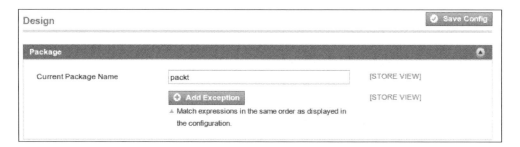

**Downloading the example code**

You can download the example code files for all Packt books you have
purchased from your account at http://www.packtpub.com. If you
purchased this book elsewhere, you can visit http://www.packtpub.
com/support and register to have the files e-mailed directly to you.

4. Save the configuration and your site will look as follows:

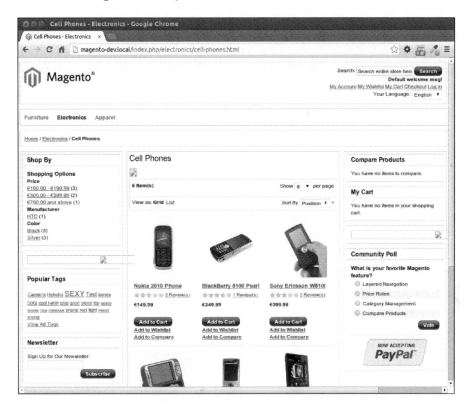

The theme is now installed and ready for further development.

## How it works...

We have just created a blank theme; a theme with only structural CSS. When we want to customize the look and feel with CSS, we have to work in the following folders and files:

- `skin/frontend/packt/default/css`
- `skin/frontend/packt/default/css/styles.css` (the main css file)
- `skin/frontend/packt/default/images` (the css images folder)

With these files, you can change the CSS look and feel of the shop. If you want to change some of the HTML code, you have to work in the `app/design/frontend/packt/default` folder.

This folder is inherited from the `app/design/frontend/base/default` folder where the standard files are stored. If you want to change a file in the `base` folder, you need to copy the file with the same folder structure from the `base` folder to your theme.

> Changing the code of the base package files will also work but this is not recommended because these files are part of the Magento core. When these files are changed, your changes will be lost after a Magento upgrade and your code maintainability becomes low.

If you want to change the `header.phtml` file that is located at `app/design/frontend/base/default/template/page/html/header.phtml`, you have to copy it to `app/design/frontend/packt/default/template/page/html/header.phtml`.

When it is located there, clear your caches. Now, the file of your theme is loaded instead of the one in the base folder.

> In the Magento development process, you have to clear the caches to see your changes. It is also possible to disable the cache. If so, you don't have to clear the cache many times when developing but you will have longer page loads.

## There's more...

To see from where every file is loaded, you can turn on **Template Path Hints**. To do this, go to the backend and navigate to **System | Configuration | Developer**.

Navigate to your store view in the top-left corner and set the following configuration:

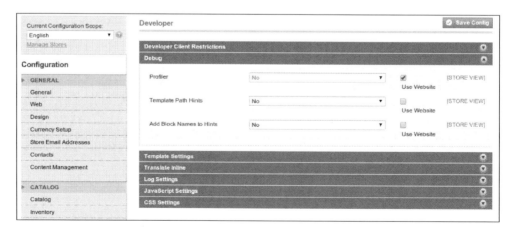

When this is set, navigate to the frontend and you will see red columns around every block.

# Adding extra files to your theme

In the previous recipe, we set up our theme with one CSS file. Mostly, you want to add some more files to it (when you are using a JavaScript plugin or something).

## Getting ready

We will add an extra CSS and JavaScript file to our theme. To do this, we have to work in the following two directories:

- `app/design/frontend/packt/default/layout`
- `skin/frontend/packt/default`

## How to do it...

In the following steps, we will see how we can add extra files to a theme:

1. Copy the `page.xml` file. The declarations of all the CSS and JavaScript files that need to be included are stored in the file `app/design/frontend/base/default/layout/page.xml`.

    It is possible that there are other CSS and JavaScript declarations in other layout XML files. The `page.xml` file is used to set up the default layout structure.

2. We need to add something. So we need to copy this file with the same folder structure to our theme folder. Copy the file to `app/design/frontend/packt/default/layout/page.xml`.

3. Add the CSS declaration.

4. If you open the `page.xml` file and look in the `<default>` tag, you will see a lot of lines with `"addCss"`. We need to add the following line in that section:

   `<action method="addCss"><stylesheet>css/packt.css</stylesheet></action>`

    The path we specify here is the path starting from our theme root folder, so it is `css/packt.css`. Magento will use the theme fallback to find the file in the `theme`, `package`, or `base` folder.

5. Don't forget to create the CSS file. Create the `packt.css` file in the `skin/frontend/packt/default/css/` folder.

6. Clear the Magento cache.

 When you change something in the XML files, you will always have to clear the cache to see the effect of your changes. It is also possible to disable the cache. The purpose is that you don't have to clear the cache many times as the page loads are slower.

7. Reload the frontend and look at the HTML source. Your file should be added.

## How it works...

The `addCss` function is one of the functions in the head block of Magento. This block will generate the HTML head section of a page.

The following functions are useful when working with extra CSS and JS files:

▶ `addJs`: This function will add a JS file from the `js` folder (folder in the root directory) to the head of the page.

▶ `addItem`: This is a function that will add a JS or CSS file to the head of the page. The function has two required parameters: the type and the filename.

The type can have the following values:

▶ `skin_js`: This is a JavaScript file in the `skin` folder

▶ `js_css`: This is a CSS file in the `js` folder

▶ `js`: This is a JavaScript file in the `js` folder

▶ `css`: This is a CSS file in the `skin` folder

▶ `rss`: This creates a `<link>` HTML tag with an attribute `type="application/rss+xml"`

The `addItem` function has three other optional parameters to customize the output of the tag in the `head` tag.

## There's more...

When you use the right functions to include images, JavaScript, and CSS, you have the following advantages over adding HTML code in a `.phtml` file:

▶ You can merge the CSS and JavaScript files to one file when you configure it

- ▸ It always contains the right absolute URL to the file (it contains the right domain and protocol)
- ▸ It uses the theme fallback system

# Adding jQuery support

Magento 1.8 and earlier versions didn't use jQuery in the frontend and backend. The library that Magento uses for the JavaScript functionality is Prototype. When you want to use some jQuery code, you need to add the jQuery library in your theme.

## Getting ready

Go to the jQuery website and get the latest version.

## How to do it...

By default, Magento loads the Prototype library. Excluding this will cause JavaScript errors on every page, so we need to use both libraries. The problem with jQuery and Prototype is that they both use the dollar sign ($) as the namespace for their functions.

To avoid the conflict, we have to use jQuery in the noconflict mode:

1. Put the jQuery library in the `js/jquery` folder.
2. We will create a `local.xml` file in our theme folder to add extra layout instructions. Create the `app/design/frontend/packt/default/local.xml` file.
3. Add the following content in that file:

```xml
<?xml version="1.0" encoding="UTF-8"?>
<layout>
  <default>
    <reference name="head">
      <action method="addJs">
        <js>jquery/jquery.js</js>
      </action>
    </reference>
  </default>
</layout>
```

4. Create a `jquery.noconflict.js` file in the `js/jquery` folder with the following content:

```
$.noConflict();
```

5. Add this file, after adding the jQuery file, in your `local.xml` file. The file contains the following code snippet:

```xml
<?xml version="1.0" encoding="UTF-8"?>
<layout>
  <default>
    <reference name="head">
      <action method="addJs">
        <js>jquery/jquery.js</js>
      </action>
      <action method="addJs">
        <js>jquery/jquery.noconflict.js</js>
      </action>
    </reference>
  </default>
</layout>
```

6. Clear your caches and look at the source of your frontend.

7. The jQuery file and the `noconflict` file should be added in the head section.

8. You can now use jQuery in your webshop.

> Keep in mind that you have to call jQuery with the `jQuery` namespace instead of the `$` namespace.
>
> Also keep in mind that third-party extensions of Magento could include jQuery in the frontend. Make sure the version is compatible with your code.

9. We normally use the following code snippet:

```
$(document).ready(function() {});
```

But, we will instead use the following line with the jQuery namespace:

```
jQuery(document).ready(function () {});
```

## How it works...

We added two files to the theme that contains the jQuery library. We had to use the noconflict mode to avoid conflicts with the prototype library.

To add files to the layout, we created a `local.xml` file. In that file, we added instructions to add the JavaScript files to the head of the HTML code.

The main advantage of using a `local.xml` file for this is that you don't have to overwrite an entire XML file from the base folder to add just two lines of code.

# Changing a page title

In the previous chapter, we added some CSS and JavaScript files to the `<head>` tag of the HTML. To change the page title, we have to do it in a similar way.

We will change the page title of the contacts page that is available at `http://magento-dev.local/contacts`.

## How to do it...

To change the page title of the contacts page, have a look at the following steps:

1. Go to the contacts page in the frontend. This is available at `http://magento-dev.local/contacts`.

2. You see that the page title reads **Contact Us**. We will change this to **Give us a message**.

3. Copy the `layout/contacts.xml` file from the base theme to our theme and open the file. In this file, there is an xml tag `<contacts_index_index>`:

```
<contacts_index_index translate="label">
  <label>Contact Us Form</label>
  <reference name="head">
    <action method="setTitle" translate="title" module="contacts">
<title>Contacts Us</title></action>
  </reference>
  <reference name="root">
    <action method="setTemplate"><template>page/2columns-
    right.phtml</template></action>
    <action method="setHeaderTitle" translate="title"
    module="contacts"><title>Contact Us</title></action>
  </reference>
  <reference name="content">
    <block type="core/template" name="contactForm"
    template="contacts/form.phtml"/>
  </reference>
</contacts_index_index>
```

4. In the `<reference name="head">` tag, you will see a `setTitle` method. Set this line as follows:

```
<action method="setTitle" translate="title"
module="contacts"><title>Give us a message</title></action>
```

5. Clear your cache and reload the page. The title in your browser is now changed to **Give us a message.**

## How it works...

The `<title>` tag in the HTML page is in the head section. This head section is generated by the Magento head block.

In the template file, the code looks as follows:

```
<title><?php echo $this->getTitle() ?></title>
```

This means that Magento will print the title of that object in the tag. To set the title of that object, we use the `setTitle` function.

# Working with translations

Magento has the ability to run multiple stores in different languages. In the sample store, you can see English, French, and a German store view.

## Getting ready

Open the backend and go to the general configuration section (**System | Configuration | General**). We will configure the languages for the store views and do some inline translations.

## How to do it...

The following steps show you how you can translate strings in a Magento store:

1. Configure the languages for each store view.
2. At the top-left corner, you will see a store switcher where you can switch the configuration for a store. Set the French language for the French store view and the German language for the German store view.
3. Clear the cache and reload your frontend.

 You will see no changes because there is no language pack installed by default for French and German. Language packs are available in Magento Connect.

4.  Enable the inline translation. We will translate our store with the inline translation tool that you can configure from **System | Configuration | Developer** (the last tab). In the default configuration scope, configure the following:

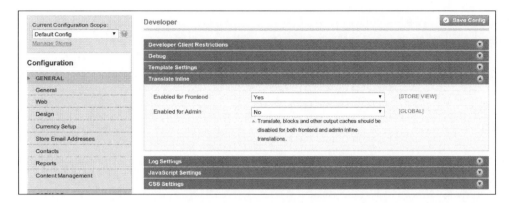

5.  Reload your frontend. You will see red frames around a lot of strings in the frontend. When you hover and click on the icon, a pop-up window will show the translation form:

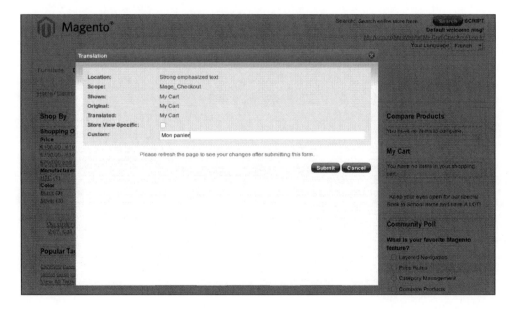

With this translation form, you can create your own translations for the language of the current store.

6.  Click on **Submit**, clear the caches, and reload the page.

If everything goes well, you will see that the text is translated into the string you just entered. Make sure you always clear the cache when editing a translation.

## How it works...

Magento has a very powerful translate function. To create a string in this translate function, you have to use the following syntax:

```
Mage::helper('core')->__('Text to translate');
```

This syntax always works, but when working in template files, you can also use the shorter syntax:

```
$this->__('Text to translate');
```

The translate function will search for the string in the following ways:

- ▶ First, Magento will look into the `core_translate` table of the database. In this table, only those translations which you have translated inline are added (like we did in this recipe).

- ▶ If no matching string is found in the `core_translate` table, Magento will look at the `translate.csv` file in the theme. This file is located under `app/design/frontend/<<my_package>>/<<my_theme>>/locale/<<language>>/translate.csv`.

- ▶ If the string is not found in the theme translation file, Magento will search for the string in the `app/locale/<<language>>` folder. In this folder, you can find all the translation files. A translate package will contain some of the module's translate files (`.csv`).

- ▶ If no string is found in the module's translate files, Magento will print the original string that is passed as an argument to the translation function.

# Understanding the theming block system

The Magento frontend is not a single file. It is a combination of blocks nested in each other. Each block is an object you can play with.

## Getting ready

Open a category page in your shop and you see a lot of frames which all represent a block. Some blocks are structural (left column, right column, content, and footer) and others contain content (product list, cart, navigation, and so on).

## How to do it...

In the next two steps, we will enable the frontend hints to get an idea of the used blocks on a page.

1. Enable your frontend **Template Path Hints**. Go to **System | Configuration | Developer** and enable the template and block names.

2. Reload the frontend. When the frontend hints are enabled, a frontend page will have red frames around each block.

Each block with a template is in a red frame. The title in white is the template file and the blue title is the classname of the block object.

When you want to edit the content of a block, you will have to look at the files displayed in the red frames. Make sure when a template file is in the base theme, you copy it to your theme.

## How it works...

All the blocks are declared in layout XML files. These layout files are stored in the layout folder of a theme.

When you open a layout file, everything is stored in the layout XML tag. The children of this tag are layout handles.

A layout handle is a set of layout instructions that can be loaded on a page. When you look at the `contacts.xml` file, you see two handles. Layout handles are always in the second level of the `<layout>` XML tree:

- `default`
- `contacts_index_index`

The default handle will be loaded on every page. The `contacts_index_index` handle will be loaded on the contacts page.

When you want to load a layout instruction on a page, you have to name your handle as follows:

```
<modulename>_<controllername>_<actionname>
```

For the contacts page, you have to enter following values:

- Module: `contacts`
- Controller: `IndexController`
- Action: `indexAction`

For the login page, it is as follows:

- ▸ Module: `customer`
- ▸ Controller: `AccountController`
- ▸ Action: `loginAction`

So, the name of the handle is `customer_account_login`.

You can find more information about controllers and their actions in the *Adding a new page* recipe in *Chapter 4, Creating a Module*.

When you look at the `customer.xml` file in the theme, you will see this handle with the instructions for the login page. When you look inside a handle, you will see the `<reference>` tags. Inside these tags, you see the `<block>` tags.

A reference is a block. When you have `<reference name="left">`, you are performing actions in the block with the name `left`. This block with the name `left` is declared in the `page.xml` file of the theme.

Actions that you can perform are as follows:

- ▸ Calling methods on the block object with `<action method="methodName">`
- ▸ Adding child blocks
- ▸ Removing child blocks
- ▸ Setting a template

The Magento frontend is built with blocks. The main block where everything starts from is called root. If you look at the `page.xml` file in our theme, in the default handle, you will see how the structural blocks are initialized.

# Adding widgets to the layout

In the previous recipe, we described the Magento layout blocks. Writing layout XML files is not so easy as there is a graphical interface to add blocks to the layout. This interface is called **widgets**.

## Getting ready

We will add a product link to the left column of the category page. Go to the backend and navigate to **CMS | Widgets**.

# How to do it...

In the following steps, we will configure a widget for the category pages.

1. Choose **Add new widget instance**.

2. In the next form, choose the configuration shown in the following screenshot:

3. Click on **Continue** and the following screen shows up:

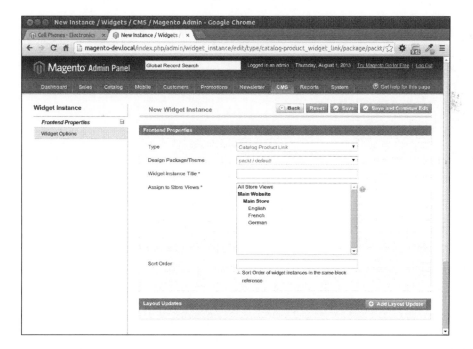

4.  Fill in the form with the following values:

    ❑ **Widget Instance Title**: `Widget-category-left-product`

    This is the title of the widget in the backend. A structural name is easy when working with a lot of widgets.

    ❑ **Assign to Store Views: All Store Views**

    In the **Widget Options** tab, you have to choose the product.

5.  Save the widget. Click on **Save and Continue Edit**. The widget instance is now saved but nothing will show up in the frontend because there is no layout update set.

6.  To show the widget in the frontend, we have to create a layout update by clicking on the **Add Layout Update** button.

7.  Fill in the form as follows:

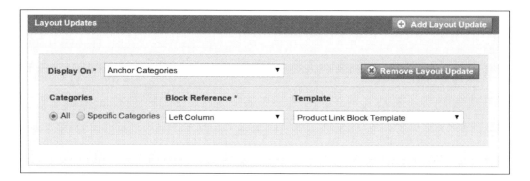

8.  Clear the cache and go to a category page. A product link will show up in the left column.

## How it works...

In the left column, a new block is added to the frontend. Like each block on the frontend, this widget has a block class and a template similar to the other blocks.

The only difference is that this block is not generated by an XML file but by an XML layout instruction in the database.

The widget interface will generate a layout XML that is stored in the database. The block class and template are similar to other blocks in the XML files.

# Working with Products

**3**

In this chapter, we will cover:

- ▸ Setting up the catalog defaults
- ▸ Working with attribute sets
- ▸ Working with product types
- ▸ Adding a Facebook like button
- ▸ Adding a product to the cart through querystring
- ▸ Embedding a YouTube video
- ▸ Changing the URL of a product page

## Introduction

The choice of products and how they are displayed on the frontend are very important to make a web shop with good usability. Making a visitor buy something is the main target of every shop owner.

We have to set up the products in a way such that a visitor can quickly find what they are looking for. If this is done and the shop looks reliable, a visitor is more likely to buy something.

This chapter will explain all the possibilities of what you can do with a set of products and how to add extra things such as a video or a `like` button.

The goal of this chapter is to make your shop more user-friendly without a lot of development.

# Setting up the catalog defaults

The first step is to configure the catalog settings to the preferred values. We will cover all the configuration values that are possible with a standard installation.

## Getting ready

Open the frontend in a tab of your browser. In the second tab, open the backend and log in.

## How to do it...

In the next steps, we will configure the settings of the catalog (category and product) pages:

1. Go to the **Configuration** section in **System**, and click on the **Catalog** tab. You will see the following screen:

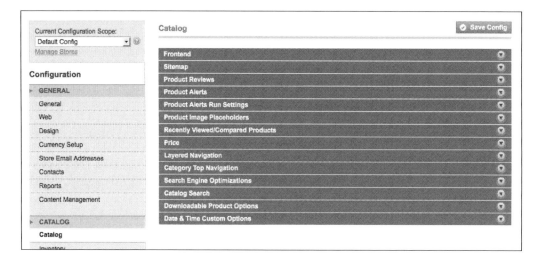

2. Open the frontend section and set the following values:

   ❑ **List mode**: grid (Show products by default in a grid or list)

   ❑ **Products per page on Grid allowed values: 12,24,36**

   ❑ **Products per page on Grid default value: 24**

While changing the allowed and default value for a grid page, make sure the numbers are divisible by the number of products in a row. Otherwise, the number of products on a page will not fit in the grid.

- ❑ **Products per page on List allowed values**: 10,20,30,40
- ❑ **Products per page on List default value**: 10
- ❑ **Allow all products per page**: No

 When you have a large number of products, it is not recommended to set the **Allow all products per page** option to **Yes**. When you have 2,000 products, and you want to show all the products on a single page, you will generate an enormous HTML output that can cause memory issues.

- ❑ **Product listing Sort by**: price
- ❑ **Use Flat Catalog Category**: No
- ❑ **Use Flat Catalog Product**: No

 The purpose of the preceding two settings (**Use Flat Catalog Category** and Use Flat Catalog Product) is explained in the *Working with EAV tables* recipe in *Chapter 5, Database Concepts*.

- ❑ **Allow Dynamic Media URLs in Products and Categories**: Yes

3. Set the following values under the **Sitemap** section:

- ❑ **Use tree like category sitemap**: Yes
- ❑ **Minimum lines per page**: 30

This setting will change the look of the sitemap pages. You can find this at `catalog/seo_sitemap/category`.

4. Enable the product reviews for guests. This allows everyone to write a review about a product. When this is enabled, a review form will appear on the product review page.

5. Open the **Product Alert Settings** section to configure product alert e-mails that will be sent when the price or stock changes.

We will configure a stock alert with the following settings:

- ❑ **Allow alert when product price changes**: No
- ❑ **Allow alert when product stock changes**: Yes

 The previous configurations will send stock alert e-mails (a stock alert is triggered when a product becomes available in stock) to the subscribed e-mail addresses.

6. We can set the **Product Alert Run Settings** values in the next section. We will configure a daily job at 0400 hours to send the alert e-mails:

   ❑ **Frequency: Daily**

   ❑ **Start time: 04:00:00**

7. Leave the product image placeholders as they are. Here, we can set a default image that will be shown when a product has no image or the image is not found. The best way is to set the placeholder image(s) in the theme.

8. In the **Recently Viewed/Compared Products** tab, set the following values:

   ❑ **Show for current: Website**

 This will show the recent products you viewed over all stores and store views in the website.

   ❑ **Default recently viewed count: 5**

   ❑ **Default recently compared count: 5**

9. In the **Price** tab, set **Catalog Price Scope** as **Global**. For this tutorial, we don't need different prices for each store view. When **Price Scope** is set to **Global**, we can only configure one price for a product in different store views.

10. In the **Layered Navigation** section, we will modify some settings to customize the left navigation for the category pages.

    ❑ **Display product count: Yes**

    ❑ **Price ranges: Equalize price ranges**

    By setting this, the price steps will always have the same increment.

11. Set the top navigation **Category** to **3**. This will mean that the depth of the navigation is three levels at the maximum.

12. Skip the **Search Engine Optimization** option. We will look into it in the *Changing the URL of a product page* recipe

13. Configure the **Catalog / Search** section as follows:

    ❑ **Minimal query length: 3**

    ❑ **Maximum query length: 128**

    ❑ **Maximum query words count: 10**

    ❑ **Search type: Like**

    You can set this to full text that has better results, but the performance is not so good. The previous settings configure the search behavior of Magento.

14. Don't forget to save the configuration.

## How it works...

All these settings are saved in the configuration table of Magento. The frontend files of the catalog pages will pick up these settings and render the output based on these settings.

When you add extra functionality to the category page, you can easily extend the configuration with extra parameters. More information about extending the configurations is explained in the *Extending the system configuration recipe of Chapter 7, Magento Backend*.

# Working with attribute sets

Magento has a flexible system to work with products. When you sell, for example, a board game and a computer, the specifications of each product are different. Suppose I want to configure an age for the board game and a screen resolution for the computer. In such cases, these things are covered with **attributes** and **attribute sets**.

When you create a product, you have to first select an attribute set (with specific attributes) before entering other data.

## Getting ready

Go to the backend and navigate to **Catalog | Attributes | Manage Attributes** and **Catalog | Attributes | Manage Attribute Sets**.

We will create some extra attributes and an attribute set on these pages.

## How to do it...

In the next steps, we will create extra product attributes that we can use with an attribute set:

1. Create a new attribute on the **Manage Attributes** page.
2. After you click on **New Attribute**, fill in the form as follows:
   - **Attribute Code: available_from** (the code of the attribute used in the database and functions)
   - **Scope: Store View** (this setting adds the ability to specify a separate value for each store view)
   - **Catalog Input Type for Store Owner: Date** (this is the type of the attribute)
   - **Default Value**: empty
   - **Unique Value: No**
   - **Values Required: No**

- ❑ **Apply To**: **All Product Types**

- ❑ **Use in Quick Search**: **No** (this option searches through the attribute values while performing a quick search)

- ❑ **Use in Advanced Search**: **No** (this option makes the attribute available to search on in the **Advanced search** option)

- ❑ **Comparable on Front end**: **No** (this option shows the attribute in the product comparing tool)

- ❑ **Use for Promo Rule Conditions**: **No**

- ❑ **Position**: empty

- ❑ **Visible on Product View Page on Front-end**: **Yes** (this option shows the attribute value on product pages)

- ❑ **Used in Product Listing**: **No** (this option makes the attribute value available on category pages)

- ❑ **Used for sorting in Product Listing**: **No** (this option makes the attribute available to sort on category pages)

3. In the **Manage Label / Options** field, fill in the labels for the frontend.

4. Click on **Save Attribute** and the attribute is saved.

5. Create a new attribute set by navigating to **Catalog | Attributes | Manage Attribute Sets**.

6. Fill in the form as follows and click on **Save Attribute Set**:

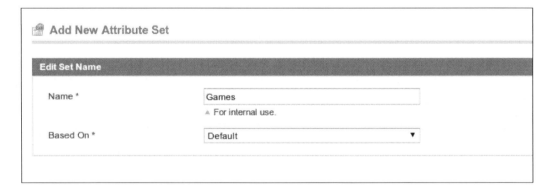

7. The attribute set overview opens. On this page, you can drag-and-drop the attributes in the appropriate groups.

8.  Create a group named `Game specific data` and drag the **available_from**, **memory**, and **processor** attributes to it.

    The overview will look as follows:

9.  Save the attribute set.

10. Create a new product in **Manage Products** from **Catalog**, and enter the following configuration:

    □   **Attribute Set: Games**

    □   **Product Type: Simple Product**

11. Click on **Continue**.

You will see that the special game attributes are now available in the **Game specific data** tab:

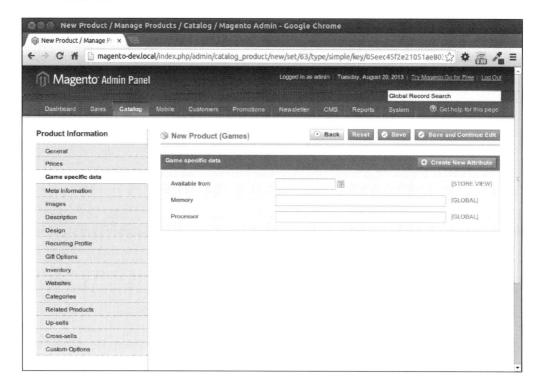

Attributes and attribute sets are used when you work with multiple families of products. In the sample data of our shop, there are more attribute sets available for cameras, computers, shirts, shoes, and more.

With attribute sets, you can group attributes of a family with each other.

While creating a new attribute, you will have to specify the type of the attribute. The following types are available with different inputs and outputs:

- **Text field**
- **Text area** (a text field with multiple lines)
- **Date**
- **Yes / No**
- **Multiple Select**

- ▸ **Dropdown**
- ▸ **Price**
- ▸ **Media Image**
- ▸ **Fixed Product Tax** (this is used for extra taxes such as author taxes)

 When you will use an attribute as a filter in the left navigation on the category pages, this attribute must have the type **Dropdown**, **Multiple Select**, or **Price**.

# Working with product types

In Magento, there are different types of products you can create. The standard product is a simple product. This type of product is used to sell basic products. However, there are other product types where you can choose options or a size.

## Getting ready

We will create a configurable product. For example, you want to buy a pair of shoes where you can choose their size and color. Open your backend and navigate to **Catalog | Manage Products**.

## How to do it...

In the following steps, we will create a product (shoes) where we can specify their sizes on the product detail page:

1. Choose the following configuration when you hit the **Add Product** button:

2. When we click on **Next**, we have to choose the attributes to configure. This product has to be configurable on the **Shoe size** attribute. Select the checkbox and click on **Continue**.

3. Fill in the required attributes, and save the product by clicking on **Save And Continue Edit**.

 To make a product visible in the store, check the **Websites**, **Status**, **Visibility**, **Category**, and **Inventory** attributes.

4. Navigate to the **Associated Products** tab where we will create the child products.

5. By adding the following configuration to the **Quick simple product creation** section, we will add five child products:

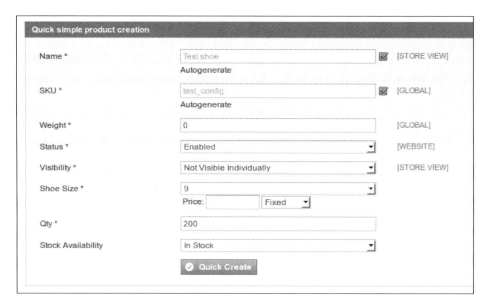

6. Click on the **Quick Create** button and repeat this four times with a different shoe size.

7. When everything goes well, the **Super product attributes configuration** section will look as follows:

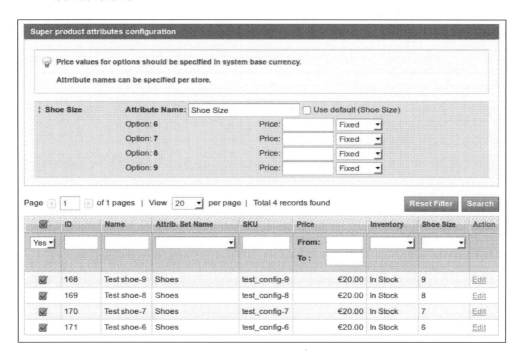

8. Click on the **Save And Continue** button and the product is saved.

9. Navigate to the frontend and search for the product we just created. When we are on the product detail page, you will see a dropdown where you can choose the options we have just created.

## How it works...

A configurable product is a product in which you will have to configure the options before adding it to the cart. The customer will see the configurable product in the cart, but in the background a simple product is also added to the cart.

That's the reason we have to create simple products to use as options for the configurable product. The configurable product is the parent that is used to show the child products in the frontend. When a product is sold, the SKU of the selected child product will be used to process the order. That's the reason the stock is configured on the child products.

## There's more...

In Magento, you can create six types of products. The following section gives a short description of what is possible with the different product types.

### Simple product

A simple product is just a product that you can sell in your web shop. Every product in Magento has a unique ID (**SKU**) that mostly has the same value as the article code of the suppliers.

### Configurable product

In this recipe, we created a configurable product. This product has child products that you can configure on the product detail page (for example, to configure the size). The child products are simple products.

### Bundled product

A bundled product is like a configurable product, but with this one you can specify more (optional) options. For a good example of a bundled product, you can go to **Electronics | Computers | Build Your Own**. The products in this category are bundled products.

### Grouped product

A grouped product is a product that represents a set where you can specify the number of child products. A good example of this can be found in **Furniture | Magento Red Furniture Set**.

### Virtual product

A virtual product is like a simple product but it is not physical. It has no inventory and can't be shipped. In the sample data, the warranties on the bundled products of the sample store are good examples of virtual products.

### Downloadable product

A downloadable product is a product that is not physical. When a customer buys a product like this, they will receive a download link where they can download their product such as a PDF, ZIP, MP3, or any other type of file.

# Adding a Facebook like button

These days, it is trendy to show a Facebook `like` button on your website so that visitors can share the page with their friends.

In this recipe, we will add the `like` button on every product page.

## Getting ready

Open your browser and go to a product page. In your IDE, open your configured theme folder.

## How to do it...

In the next steps, we will generate and add the code of a Facebook `like` button to the product detail pages:

1. Open the `catalog/product/view.phtml` template from your theme. If it is not in the theme, copy it from the `app/design/frontend/base/default` folder.

2. Go to `http://developers.facebook.com/docs/reference/plugins/like` from where you can use the **Configurator** page to customize the `like` button for your page, as shown in the following screenshot:

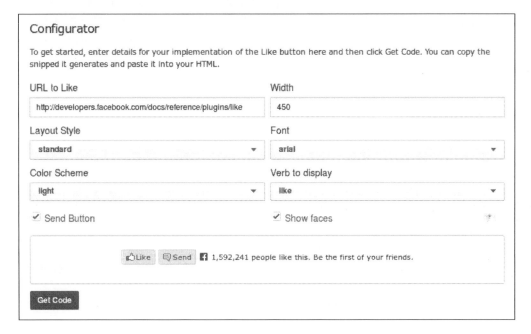

3. Paste the code in your `view.phtml` file where it will be more readable; for example, at the end of the file as a child of the `div` tag with the class `product-collateral`.

4. Reload a product page and the `like` button will show up.

5. To change the URL of the `like` button, change the `data-href` attribute of the HTML5 code. The following code shows you how to do this to use the product page URL:

```
<div class="fb-like"
    data-href="<?php echo Mage::helper('core/url')
    ->getCurrentUrl() ?>"
    data-layout="standard"
    data-action="like"
    data-show-faces="true"
    data-share="true">
</div>
```

6. While using the HTML5 code, don't forget to include the JavaScript SDK.

## How it works...

The Facebook `like` button is one of the social plugins you can embed in your website. On Facebook, every URL is an object you can like or comment on. You can find more information about the available social plugins from the following URL:

`https://developers.facebook.com/docs/plugins/`

In this recipe, we covered the addition of the Facebook `like` button, but when you want to add buttons for other social media sites such as Twitter or Google Plus, you can visit the following URLs:

▶ `https://developers.google.com/+/web/+1button/`

▶ `https://about.twitter.com/resources/buttons`

## There's more...

When you like a page of your website, Facebook will generate a wall post based on the HTML markup of the page. When you like a page, Facebook will post an image, title, and description of that item on your wall.

With **Open Graph** (**og**) `meta` tags, you can customize the content of these things. An overview of the available og tags and how to use them can be found at `https://developers.facebook.com/docs/opengraph/using-objects/`.

# Adding a product to the cart through querystring

In some use cases, you will link a visitor to your site when they directly add a product to the cart; for example, when you have a campaign with a **buy now** button on an external website.

## Getting ready

Open your browser with your shop and navigate to **Catalog | Manage Products** in the backend.

## How to do it...

In the next steps, we will create a URL where a product will be added to the cart:

1. Find a product in your frontend you want to add to the cart. For example, navigate to **Furniture | Living Room | Ottoman**.

2. Find this product in the backend and keep the ID in mind.

3. To add a product, we have to call the `checkout/cart/add` URL with the product ID as the GET parameter. So, the final URL will be `http://magento-dev.local/checkout/cart/add?product=51`.

4. While calling this URL, you will be redirected to the cart page with one item of this product in the cart.

5. When you add the `qty` parameter to the query, you can add more than one item of the same product to the cart. Call the `http://magento-dev.local/checkout/cart/add?product=51&qty=3` URL, and you will see that three products are added to the cart.

> It is not possible to add two or more different products to the cart with the same query. If you want to do this, you can create a grouped product.

## How it works...

If we monitor the `add to cart` action in our shop, we will see that there is a GET or POST request to the `checkout/cart/add` action in the frontend. This action will forward the request to the cart page if it is valid.

Adding a simple product is easy, but if we want to add a grouped, configurable, or bundled product, the querystring is a bit more complex.

To know which parameters you have to send to the add action, we have to debug this with Firebug. In the **Net Panel**, as shown in the following screenshot, you can debug the request:

The preceding screenshot shows the POST parameters of a configurable product.

# Embedding a YouTube video

In a product description, we can add HTML tags so that we can use the <object> tag to embed a YouTube video in the description of a product.

## Getting ready

Go to http://www.youtube.com, and choose a video that you want to add to the description of the product.

## How to do it...

The next steps show you how to embed a YouTube video on a product detail page:

1. On the YouTube video page, click on the **Embed** button. When you click on this button, the following screen shows up:

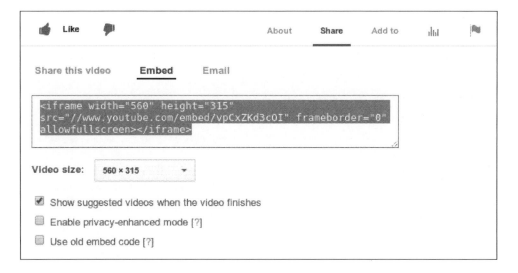

2. Copy the HTML code and paste it in the description of a product.

3. Save the product.

4. Go to the product in the frontend. You will see the video on the product page.

## How it works...

The ability to use HTML tags in product descriptions gives a lot of flexibility for this field. It is possible to use a **WYSIWYG** editor for the content because this allows us to use widgets such as a YouTube video or other third-party widgets.

# Changing the URL of a product page

When you are on a product page, the URL of every product always looks clean. The name in the URL makes it very SEO friendly.

In this recipe, we will explore the possibilities with **URL rewrites** in Magento and how it works.

## Getting ready

Go to the **Manage Products** page from **Catalog** in the backend. Open a product and have a look at the **URL key** attribute. This recipe is based on the **HTC Touch Diamond** product.

## How to do it...

In the next steps, the way you can change the URL of a product page is shown:

1. Find the appropriate product in the frontend and look for the URL. In this case, this will be `/htc-touch-diamond.html`.

2. In the backend, change the **URL key** attribute to **buy-now-htc-touch-diamond**.

3. Reload the product in the frontend. The URL will change to the new one we have entered at the backend.

>  When you select the **Create Permanent Redirect for old URL** checkbox, Magento will create a permanent 301 redirect response for the old URL of the product. The checkbox is located in the product's **Edit** page under the **URL key** attribute.

4. Empty the **URL key** attribute at the backend and save the product again. You will see that Magento autogenerates the **URL key** value based on the name of the product.

5. At the backend, go to **System | Configuration | Catalog | Search Engine Optimizations**. Empty the **Product URL Suffix** field and save the configuration.

6. Clear the cache by navigating to **System | Cache Management**.

7. Reindex the **Product URL Rewrites** index by navigating to **System | Index Management**. In the reindexing process, the URLs will be generated in the `core_url_rewrite` database table.

8. Reload the product in the frontend, and you will see that the `.html` suffix is gone.

## How it works...

In Magento, there is a URL rewrite system that maps an SEO-friendly URL to the system URL for that request. You can see all the URL rewrites in the backend. Navigate to **Catalog | URL Rewrite Management**, and you will see the complete list of URLs that Magento will map on a controller action. For example, when we search for `htc-touch-diamond`, we will see a list with all the URLs for this key.

What we see is the following:

▶ Permanent 301 redirect responses (rows where the **Options** column has the value **RP**. RP stands for Redirect Permanently.)

▶ The product URL.

▶ The category product URL.

All URLs are generated again for each store view. When a product is enabled in multiple stores, it is normal that a product has more than one URLs.

## There's more...

On the URL rewrite page, it is also possible to add custom URL rewrites; for example, a URL rewrite for the contacts page.

While adding the configuration as shown in the following screenshot, you will create a rewrite for /sitemap.html for the English store view:

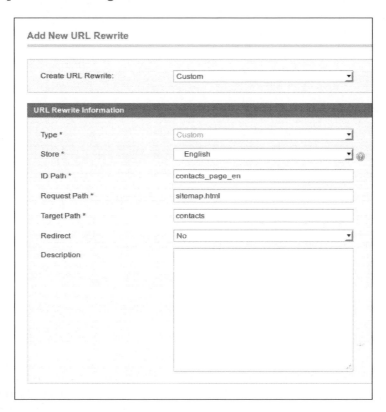

- ▶ In the **Store** dropdown, you can configure the store for the URL rewrite.
- ▶ In the **ID Path** field, the ID of the URL rewrite is set. You have to enter a unique name for this.
- ▶ The value in the **Request Path** field is the path you want to rewrite. In this case, we want to rewrite something on the /sitemap.html path.
- ▶ The value in the **Target Path** field is the path where the request will end. In this case, it is the **contacts** page.
- ▶ If the value in the **Redirect** dropdown is set to **Yes**, you can choose for a 301 redirect to the target. When it is set to **No**, the target page will be rendered on the request path (so the URL of the page doesn't change).

# 4

# Creating a Module

In this chapter, we will cover the following topics:

- ▸ Creating files
- ▸ Registering blocks, helpers, and models
- ▸ Adding a new page
- ▸ Adding a layout file
- ▸ Adding a translation file
- ▸ Adding a block of new products
- ▸ Rewriting a core class

## Introduction

When you take a look into the core code of Magento, you will see the modular architecture. Every concept is stored in a module. Magento is the combination of all the core modules. The advantage of a modular architecture is its extendibility. It is easy to add modules that extend or rewrite the core.

In this chapter, we will create a module using the most important things you need to know to extend Magento with a simple module.

## Creating files

When you want to create a module, the first step is to create the files and folders to register the module. At the end of this recipe, we will have a module that is registered but does not have functionality.

## Getting ready

Open your IDE and navigate to the `app/code/local` folder. If the local folder is not there, create the `app/code/local` folder.

## How to do it...

In the following steps, we will create the files required to register a Magento module.

1.  Create the module in `app/code/local` by creating the following folders:

    ❏   `app/code/local/Packt`

    ❏   `app/code/local/Packt/Helloworld`

    ❏   `app/code/local/Packt/Helloworld/etc`

    `Packt` is the namespace of the module and `Helloworld` is the name of the module.

2.  Register the module by creating the `Packt_Helloworld.xml` file in the `app/etc/modules` folder. Add the following content in this file:

    ```xml
    <?xml version="1.0"?>
    <config>
      <modules>
        <Packt_Helloworld>
          <active>true</active>
          <codePool>local</codePool>
        </Packt_Helloworld>
      </modules>
    </config>
    ```

3.  Create the main configuration file `config.xml` in the `etc` folder of the module. Add the following content in the file:

    ```xml
    <?xml version="1.0" encoding="UTF-8"?>
    <config>
      <modules>
        <Packt_Helloworld>
          <version>0.0.1</version>
        </Packt_Helloworld>
      </modules>
    </config>
    ```

4.  Check the registration of the module by going to the backend. Go to **System |
    Configuration | Advanced** and check whether the module is present in the list. Make
    sure that you have cleared the Magento caches.

> When running the command `wiz module-list` in your command line,
> you will see a list of all the modules, including the version, code pool,
> and more. You can find more information about the Wiz command-line
> tool in the *Configuring the development tools* recipe in *Chapter 1, Getting
> Started with Magento*.

## How it works...

Magento has three code pools. They are listed as follows:

*   **Core**: The core pool contains the modules and classes of the Magento code. It is not
    recommended to change files in this directory because this will be overwritten when
    Magento is upgraded.
*   **Community**: The community pool is for the Magento modules that are delivered
    by the community. They are mostly the free modules that you can download from
    Magento Connect.
*   **Local**: The local pool is for the custom modules such as the one we have created in
    this recipe.

The first pool where Magento will search for the code is the local code pool. Next, it will look in
the community code pool, and at last it will look in the core code pool.

# Registering blocks, helpers, and models

When we want to perform operations on our module, we have to use blocks, models, and
helpers. In this recipe we will register these object types with the right class prefix.

## Getting ready

Open the `config.xml` file of the `Packt_Helloworld` module. This file is located at `app/
code/local/Packt/Helloworld/etc/config.xml`.

## How to do it...

In the following steps, we will add configuration to the module to register the blocks, helpers, and models:

1. Register the blocks by adding the following configuration in the `config.xml` file. Add the following XML code as a child of the `<config>` tag:

```
<global>
  <blocks>
    <helloworld>
      <class>Packt_Helloworld_Block</class>
    </helloworld>
  </blocks>
</global>
```

2. Create the `app/code/local/Packt/Helloworld/Block` folder.

3. Repeat step 1 and step 2 to register the helpers and models. Your global tag will look similar to the code shown as follows:

```
<global>
  <blocks>
    <helloworld>
      <class>Packt_Helloworld_Block</class>
    </helloworld>
  </blocks>
  <helpers>
    <helloworld>
      <class>Packt_Helloworld_Helper</class>
    </helloworld>
  </helpers>
  <models>
    <helloworld>
      <class>Packt_Helloworld_Model</class>
    </helloworld>
  </models>
</global>
```

4. Create the `app/code/local/Packt/Helloworld/Helper` and `app/code/local/Packt/Helloworld/Model` folders.

5. Create the helper class of the module by adding the following content to the `app/code/local/Packt/Helloworld/Helper/Data.php` file:

```
<?php
class Packt_Helloworld_Helper_Data extends Mage_Core_Helper_
Abstract
```

```
    {

    }
```

A helper class always extends from the core helper to use the functions declared in this class.

6. Test your configuration with the Wiz command-line tool by running the following command:

```
wiz devel-models
```

You will see your registered models available in the Magento installation.

 When you change something in a configuration XML file, make sure that you clear the Magento caches before testing your configuration. Otherwise, the changes will have no effect because the old configuration is cached.

## How it works...

When these objects are registered, we can create classes in the `Block`, `Helper`, and `Model` folder. The classnames in these objects need to adhere to the following naming convention; otherwise, they can't be found:

```
<Vendor Namespace>_<Modulename>_<Objectype>_<Classname>
```

Every folder name starting with `app/code/<codepool>` is used in the classname separated by an underscore. The last part is the name of the file. Every folder or file in the `Model`, `Block`, and `Helper` folder starts with a capital letter.

Our helper class is located in `app/code/local/Packt/Helloworld/Helper`, so the classname is `Packt_Helloworld_Helper_Data`.

To load a model, we have to use the `Mage::getModel()` function. In the first parameter, we have to specify the classname, which is different from the real classname. To specify the `Packt_Helloworld_Model_Sample` class, we have to use `Mage::getModel('helloworld/sample')` to get an instance of this model.

We have registered our model as `helloworld`. The name of the model in the `Model` folder is `sample`. When you take a look at the `getModel()` function discussed previously, you see that the words `helloworld` and `sample` are in the argument of that function.

The same syntax is used to get helpers and blocks. For helpers, we have to use the `Mage::helper()` function. For blocks, this syntax is used in the layout XML files or when we use the core functions to work with blocks.

# Adding a new page

Now, we will do something visible with our module. We are going to add a page to our Magento shop, which we can use for several purposes.

## Getting ready

We have to add some configuration in the `config.xml` file and we will also create a controller file.

## How to do it...

In the following steps, we will add an extra page to the Magento installation by adding extra configurations in the `Packt_Helloworld` module:

1.  Open your IDE and navigate to the `module` folder.

2.  Add the following configuration as a child of the `config` tag in the `config.xml` file of the module:

    ```
    <frontend>
      <routers>
        <helloworld>
          <use>standard</use>
          <args>
            <module>Packt_Helloworld</module>
            <frontName>helloworld</frontName>
          </args>
        </helloworld>
      </routers>
    </frontend>
    ```

3.  To create the controller file, we will create an `IndexController.php` file in folder `app/code/local/Packt/Helloworld/controllers/`.

4.  Add the following content in this controller file. This will create two actions in the `IndexController` class:

    ```php
    <?php
    class Packt_Helloworld_IndexController extends Mage_Core_
    Controller_Front_Action
    {
      public function indexAction()
      {

      }
    ```

```
  public function helloAction()
  {
    echo 'Action hello in Helloworld IndexController';
  }
}
```

5.  Clear the cache and test the controller that is available at the following locations:

    ❑   `http://magento-dev.local/helloworld/index/hello`, for the `helloAction` function

    ❑   `http://magento-dev.local/helloworld`, for the `indexAction` function

The `helloAction()` function will display the string that we have set in the `echo` statement. The `indexAction()` function is a blank page, because we have no more code in this action.

## How it works...

The syntax of a Magento controller is shown as follows:

`<modulename or frontname>/<controllerName>/<actionName>`

In our case, module name and front name is `helloworld`, the controller name is `index`, and the action name is `hello`, so we get `/helloworld/index/hello`.

Magento recognizes the controller files when a classname ends with the word `Controller`. This is the reason why the name of the class is `IndexController`.

The same rule applies for controller actions. The function's name needs to end with the word `Action`. The part that precedes `Action` is the name of the action. A function called `helloAction()` results in the `hello` part of the URL.

 While writing names of controllers and actions, make sure you keep a track on the capital letters of the class and function names. If you miss some capital letters, your code will not work.

## There's more...

When we test the controller action, we will see a blank page. This is not wrong because there is no logic added in the controller action.

If we want to see the frontend of the shop, we have to use the following code:

```
$this->loadLayout();
$this->renderLayout();
```

This will start the layout system that will load the layout instructions. It is not always recommended to load the frontend as done in a POST action where you want to process the post and continue to the next page.

# Adding a layout file

In this recipe, we will customize the frontend of our previously created page with a custom layout XML file.

## Getting ready

For adding a layout file, we have to add some configuration in the `config.xml` file of the module and a layout XML file as well.

## How to do it...

In the following steps, we will learn how to add a layout file to the Magento module.

1. Add the following configuration to your `config.xml` file to initialize the layout XML file. Add it as a child of the `<frontend>` tag:

   ```
   <layout>
     <updates>
       <helloworld>
         <file>helloworld.xml</file>
       </helloworld>
     </updates>
   </layout>
   ```

2. Create the `helloworld.xml` file in your theme layout folder in the `app/design/frontend/<package>/<theme>/layout/helloworld.xml` directory.

3. In the `helloworld.xml` file, add the following content to test if the file is loaded:

   ```
   <?xml version="1.0" encoding="UTF-8"?>
   <layout>
     <default>
       <remove name="header" />
     </default>
   </layout>
   ```

4. Reload a page in the frontend. The previous configuration will remove the header from every page in the frontend.

5. Remove the content from the `<default>` tag and create the `helloworld_index_hello` handle in the layout XML file. You can do this by adding the following XML code as a child of the `<layout>` tag:

```
<helloworld_index_hello>

</helloworld_index_hello>
```

6. For this page, we will configure the `2columns-right` layout. To do this, add the following configuration in the layout XML file as child of the `helloworld_index_hello` handle:

```
<helloworld_index_hello>
  <reference name="root">
    <action method="setTemplate">
      <template>page/2columns-right.phtml</template>
    </action>
  </reference>
</helloworld_index_hello>
```

7. Add the following code in the `helloAction()` function of the controller to start the layout system:

```
$this->loadLayout();
$this->renderLayout();
```

8. Clear the Magento cache and navigate to the `http://magento-dev.local/helloworld/index/hello` page. You will see a page with a column towards the right-hand side.

## How it works...

If you only place a `layout.xml` file in the `app/design/frontend/<package>/<theme>/layout` folder, it will not be loaded in Magento. To do this, we have to configure it in the `config.xml` file of our module as we have done in this recipe.

The layout XML file (`helloworld.xml`) works in the same way as all other layout files work, as described in *Chapter 2, Theming*.

## There's more...

Adding a custom layout XML file adds a lot of possibilities for extending your installation. Copying an XML file to your theme and changing the required settings is the easiest way. However, if you want, add a custom layout file and manipulate the blocks in that file.

The purpose of this method is to avoid double coding. A good reference of this way of modular theming can be found at http://www.classyllama.com/development/magento-development/the-better-way-to-modify-magento-layout.

# Adding a translation file

In Magento, you can run a store in multiple languages so that your module is translatable to the configured languages. In this recipe, we will add a custom translate CSV file to our module where we can place the custom strings if needed.

## Getting ready

For this recipe, we have to add some configuration in the config.xml file of our module. Also, we have to create a translate CSV file in the locale folder.

## How to do it...

In the following steps, we will add configuration to the module so that we can translate the interface to multiple languages:

1.  Add the following configuration as a child of the <frontend> tag in the config. xml file of the helloworld module. This will initialize an extra translate file to the installation:

    ```
    <translate>
      <modules>
        <Packt_Helloworld>
          <files>
            <default>Packt_Helloworld.csv</default>
          </files>
        </Packt_Helloworld>
      </modules>
    </translate>
    ```

2.  We just configured our module to use the Packt_Helloworld.csv file. Create this file in the app/locale/en_US folder.

3.  Create a test translation in the controller. Add the following line in the indexAction() function of IndexController:

    ```
    echo $this->__('Test translation packt');
    ```

4. Go to the appropriate page (`http://magento-dev.local/helloworld`). You will see that **Test translation packt** is printed as shown in the following screenshot:

5. Add the following content in the `Packt_Helloworld.csv` file:

   ```
   "Test translation packt","Packt translation to test"
   ```

6. Clear the cache and reload the page. You will see that the output is changed to **Packt translation to test** as shown in the following screenshot:

## How it works...

Now, we will discuss the behavior of the translation function in Magento.

When calling the `__('translate string')` function, Magento will search for a translated string in the following resources:

- The `core_translate translate.csv` file in the database table, present in the `app/design/frontend/<package>/<theme>/locale` folder
- Translate files located in `app/locale/<language>`

If no matching string is found for the current language, Magento will return the string that is present in the first parameter of the `translate` function.

If a string is found in a resource, Magento won't search further for that string. That means that a string that is in the `core_translate` table and the `translate.csv` file will be loaded from the database.

The `translate` function is mostly called on the current object by using `$this->__()`, but this always refers to the `helper` function of that object. If `$this->__()` doesn't work (mostly when you are in a class that doesn't extend the abstract block, helper, or model), you have to call the `translate` function directly from the module's `helper` class as shown in the following code:

```
Mage::helper('<module name>')->__('...')
```

# Adding a block of new products

The module is now prepared for the real work. In the previous recipes, we prepared the module with the most common features. In this recipe, we will add a block of new products in our previously created page.

## Getting ready

To create a custom block, we have to create a `Block` class in the `Block` folder of the `Packt_Helloworld` module, a layout instruction to add the block to our page, and a `phtml` template in our theme to style the HTML output of the block.

## How to do it...

The following steps describe how to add a block with new products to the frontend:

1. Create the `block` class in `app/code/local/Packt/Helloworld/Block`. The name of the class is `Newproducts`, so we have to create a `Newproducts.php` file in this folder.

2. Add the following content in the file. This will create a class that extends the `Mage_Core_Block_Template` class. This class will output a template if specified:

   ```php
   <?php
   class Packt_Helloworld_Block_Newproducts extends Mage_Core_Block_
   Template
   {

   }
   ```

3. Add the template to your theme `template` folder. This is in the `app/design/frontend/<package>/<theme>/template/helloworld` folder. Create the `newproducts.phtml` file in this folder.

4. Add some HTML content such as `<h2>New Products</h2>` in this file.

5. Create a block in the `helloworld.xml` layout file by adding the following XML code in the `helloworld_index_hello` handle:

```
<reference name="content">
  <block type="helloworld/newproducts" name="block_newproducts"
  template="helloworld/newproducts.phtml" />
</reference>
```

6. Clear the cache and go to the `http://magento-dev.local/helloworld/index/hello` page. You will see the **New Products** title in the content of the site.

7. Create the `getProducts()` function in the `block` class. This function will return the five latest products from the shop. The code for the `getProducts()` function will look as follows:

```
public function getProducts()
{
    $products = Mage::getModel('catalog/product')->getCollection()
        ->addAttributeToSelect('*')
        ->setOrder('created_at')
        ->setPageSize(5);

    return $products;
}
```

In this function, we will fire a query on the product collection. We sort it by date and limit the result to 5 so that we get the latest five products.

8. Call the `getProducts()` function in the template and loop through the products to print them in a list. The template code is as follows:

```
<h2>New Products</h2>
<ul>
<?php foreach ($this->getProducts() as $_product): ?>
    <li><?php echo $_product->getName() ?></li>
<?php endforeach; ?>
</ul>
```

## How it works...

What we have done in this recipe is a basic extension of the standard Magento. We have created a custom block. This block is placed on a custom page created by the module.

In this block, there is a function that returns the five most recent products and a query is fired to get these products. This is not done by SQL, but by using the Magento collections.

The purpose of using this is to get an easy interface to return the right entities. Since a product is not stored in one database table, this saves you from programming of a very complex SQL query.

# Rewriting a core class

In some cases, you want to change something about the standard behavior of Magento. When you see some code in a core class that you want to change, you have to follow this recipe.

As it is not recommended to do changes in core files, we can rewrite the path of a class to a custom one that is a parent over the original class.

## Getting ready

In this recipe, we will rewrite the core product model to a custom class in our module.

## How to do it...

In the following steps, we will change the output of the `getName()` function of a product:

1. The `getName()` function is called on the product detail page. Navigate to this page and open the `catalog/product/view.phtml` template.

2. When you search for `getName()` in the template, you see that this is done on the `$_product` variable. To know the class of this variable, you can debug this with `echo get_class($_product)`.

3. The output of this function returns the `Mage_Catalog_Model_Product` class. To rewrite this, we have to create an empty class in our `module` folder that extends the original one. Create a `Product.php` file in the `app/code/local/Packt/Helloworld/Model/Catalog/` folder.

4. Paste the following code in that file:

```php
<?php

class Packt_Helloworld_Model_Catalog_Product extends Mage_Catalog_Model_Product {

}
```

When rewriting a class, the best practice is to follow the folder structure of the original class in your module. In the `model` folder of the `Packt_Helloworld` module, we start with a `Catalog` folder (refers to `Catalog` module). In this folder, you see the same file structure as in the original module.

5. When you clear the cache and reload the frontend, you will see that the output of the `get_class` function doesn't change. This is because we didn't add the rewrite configuration in the `config.xml` file. Open the `config.xml` file and paste the following code as a child of the `<models>` tag:

```
<catalog>
  <rewrite>
    <product>Packt_Helloworld_Model_Catalog_Product</product>
  </rewrite>
</catalog>
```

 When you want to rewrite a `block` class, you have to paste a similar configuration as a child of the `<blocks>` tag. Similarly, for `helper`, paste the configuration under the `<helpers>` tag.

6. Clear the cache and reload the product page. You will see that the output of the `get_class` function is changed to the class we have just created.

7. When the new class is loaded, it is just a case of overwriting the function you want to change in this file. When we want to change the `getName()` function, we have to add the old function in this class and change some behavior. When you paste the following code in the class, the name of the product will change:

```
public function getName()
{
    return 'Packt ' . $this->_getData('name');
}
```

8. Reload the product page and you will see that the name of the product starts with **Packt**.

## How it works...

The best practice is that you don't rewrite a core class because changing the standard behavior of Magento could break the application in some cases. A more stable method is working with event handlers that are described in *Chapter 8, Event Handlers and Cronjobs*.

Unfortunately, in some cases it isn't possible to work with events. So, you need to rewrite a core class. In this case, you have to do it as described in this recipe:

▶ Create an empty class that extends the original ones

▶ Paste the function in the class that you want to change

▶ Add the configuration in the `config.xml` file of your module to rewrite the core class

When the rewrite is added in the `config.xml` class, Magento will recognize the rewrite when the class is called with the Magento functions. For a model, this is the `Mage::getModel()` function where the first argument is the path to the model.

When calling a class directly in the code as `$product = new Mage_Catalog_Model_Product()`, the rewrite will not work because an instance is returned from the `Mage_Catalog_Model_Product` class.

# 5
# Database Concepts

In this chapter, we will cover:

- ► Finding your way in the tables
- ► Creating a database connection in Magento
- ► Working with flat tables
- ► Working with EAV tables
- ► Configuring a Master/Slave setup
- ► Repairing the database

## Introduction

Magento has a very large database model to store all kinds of information. There are many Magento modules. Every module has its own tables in the database. A naming convention is used to provide a good overview in the database. Some modules use a flat database model (one table per entity), while other modules use the **EAV (Entity Attribute Value)** database model. The recipes in this chapter will cover the most important things you need to know when you are working with a database.

## Finding your way in the tables

When you look at the tables, you will realize that the number of tables is very high. In a standard installation, there are more than 300 database tables. A structured naming convention is needed to find your way in this maze of tables.

## Getting ready

In this recipe, we will make some queries to the database to get an idea of the tables and their purpose.

Here, you have to firstly make a connection with your database client using **phpMyAdmin**.

## How to do it...

In the next steps, we will learn some methods to familiarize you with the database model in Magento:

1. Get a list of the core modules. You can do this by running the `ls -l` command in the `app/code/core/Mage` folder. This will give you the following output:

```
drwxrwxr-x   7 www-data www-data Admin
drwxrwxr-x   8 www-data www-data Adminhtml
drwxrwxr-x   6 www-data www-data AdminNotification
drwxrwxr-x   8 www-data www-data Api
drwxrwxr-x   8 www-data www-data Api2
drwxrwxr-x   7 www-data www-data Authorizenet
drwxrwxr-x   5 www-data www-data Backup
drwxrwxr-x   9 www-data www-data Bundle
drwxrwxr-x   8 www-data www-data Captcha
drwxrwxr-x   9 www-data www-data Catalog
drwxrwxr-x   5 www-data www-data CatalogIndex
drwxrwxr-x   7 www-data www-data CatalogInventory
drwxrwxr-x   6 www-data www-data CatalogRule
drwxrwxr-x   8 www-data www-data CatalogSearch
drwxrwxr-x   7 www-data www-data Centinel
drwxrwxr-x   9 www-data www-data Checkout
drwxrwxr-x  10 www-data www-data Cms
drwxrwxr-x   7 www-data www-data Compiler
drwxrwxr-x   7 www-data www-data Connect
drwxrwxr-x   7 www-data www-data Contacts
```

2. Run the SHOW TABLES command on your database. This will give the following result in phpMyAdmin:

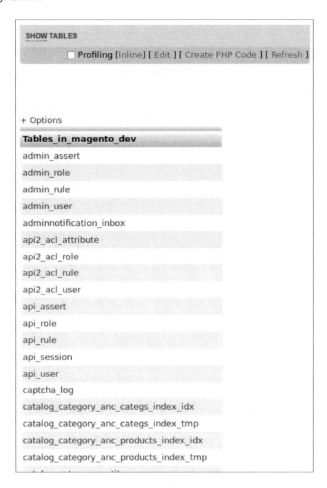

3. Compare the first part of the table names with the module list. You will see that the name of every table starts with the name of the module.

4. Go to phpMyAdmin and navigate to the **Designer** tab of the database. This page will render a database schema with all the database tables in Magento.

5.  You can limit the result by checking the tables you want to see in the left column. Uncheck all the tables and check the core tables. These are the tables starting with `core_*`. This will give you an overview of the relationships between the core tables, as shown in the following screenshot:

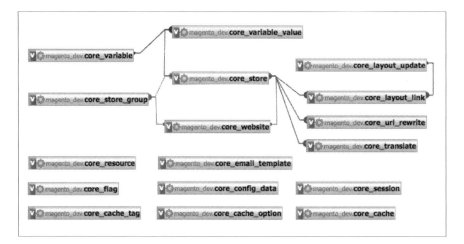

6.  In the previous screenshot, we see that there are a lot of relations starting from the `core_store` table. Let's have a look at the structure of this table. You can do this by clicking on the **Relation view** link in the **Structure** tab of the `core_store` table. This gives the following output:

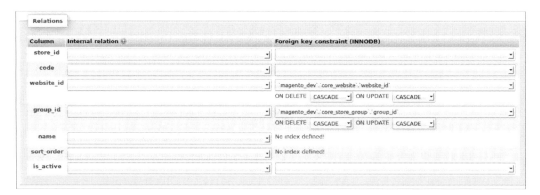

## How it works...

The Magento database is just like any database with tables and relations between them. The difficulty is that there are so many tables that make a simple overview very difficult.

You don't need to know the whole structure of the database while working. With the **Designer** option in phpMyAdmin, you can show the tables you want to see.

Most of the tables in the database represent entities in Magento. These entities (models) are connected with the database using the Magento framework. This framework uses collections to do select queries on the database. These collections will generate a `Zend_Db_Statement` object that generates SQL queries.

The purpose of these collections is that they return instances of Magento models. A SQL or Zend DB query will return an array with data.

# Creating a database connection in Magento

Magento uses resources to connect to a database. By default, Magento uses one connection to interact with the database. In this connection, there are resources declared in the `config.xml` files of the modules to link the models with the right table.

In this recipe, we will use a Magento connection to read some tables and we will learn how to configure a second connection to another database, such as a third-party system.

## Getting ready

Navigate to `IndexController` of the `Packt_Helloworld` module that we created in *Chapter 4, Creating a Module*. We will test some connections in the `indexController`.

## How to do it...

In the following steps, we will explain how to work with multiple database connections in your script:

1. Paste the following code in the `indexAction` method:

```
$resource = Mage::getSingleton('core/resource');
$connection = $resource->getConnection('core_read');

$results = $connection->query('SELECT * FROM core_store')->fetchAll();

Zend_Debug::dump($results);
```

   This query will return an array of the values in the `core_store` table.

2. Reload the `indexAction` method in the frontend. You will see all the values from the `core_store` table like the following code:

```
array(4) {
  [0] => array(7) {
```

```
    ["store_id"] => string(1) "0"
    ["code"] => string(5) "admin"
    ["website_id"] => string(1) "0"
    ["group_id"] => string(1) "0"
    ["name"] => string(5) "Admin"
    ["sort_order"] => string(1) "0"
    ["is_active"] => string(1) "1"
  }
  [1] => array(7) {
    ["store_id"] => string(1) "1"
    ["code"] => string(7) "default"
    ["website_id"] => string(1) "1"
    ["group_id"] => string(1) "1"
    ["name"] => string(7) "English"
    ["sort_order"] => string(1) "0"
    ["is_active"] => string(1) "1"
  }
  . . .
```

3. Create a new connection. For example, we will make some queries on a second Drupal database. Paste the following code in the `indexAction` method and modify the connection parameters with your credentials:

```
$dbConfig = array(
    'host' => 'localhost',
    'dbname' => 'drupal',
    'username' => 'drupal_web',
    'password' => 'drupal_pwd',
);
$_resource = Mage::getSingleton('core/resource');

//Create the connection
$connection = $_resource->createConnection('drupalConnection',
'pdo_mysql', $dbConfig);
$results = $connection->query('SELECT * FROM node')->fetchAll();

Zend_Debug::dump($results);
```

4. Reload your frontend and you will see the result of your previous query. The previous piece of code will make a connection to an external database using the Magento connection.

## How it works...

The database connections in Magento are managed by the `Mage_Core_Model_Resource` model. By using the **singleton** pattern to load the class, the connection is made once per process.

To get an instance of a model, you can use the `Mage::getModel()` function, which returns a new instance of the object. By using the `Mage::getSingleton()` function, an instance of the object given in the first parameter is returned. However, once the model is declared, Magento doesn't create a new instance but returns the existing instance of the object.

# Working with flat tables

Magento has two types of entities while working with the databases: **flat** entities and **EAV** entities.

Flat tables works with fields that represent columns in a database table. EAV tables, which are described in the next chapter, will use attributes. In this recipe, we will concentrate on flat tables.

## Getting ready

In this recipe, we will make some example queries on flat tables. Open the `IndexController` from the `Packt_Helloworld` module and create a `flatAction()` method in it. This controller action will be used to trigger the example queries.

## How to do it...

In the next set of instructions, we will show you how a flat table from the database is linked to a Magento model:

1. Have a look at the review tables. You can do this by filtering them in the phpMyAdmin table names.

2. Get all the data from the `review_detail` table. You can do this by clicking on the table.

3. Print the same data by selecting it in the Magento code. To do this, paste the following code in your `flatAction` method:

```
$resource = Mage::getSingleton('core/resource');
$connection = $resource->getConnection('core_read');

$results = $connection->query('SELECT * FROM review_detail')->fetchAll();

Zend_Debug::dump($results);
```

While executing this code, an array of values is returned.

4. We can get the same result by working with the Magento collections. You can do this by running the following code:

```
$reviews = Mage::getModel('review/review')->getCollection();

foreach ($reviews as $_review) {
    Zend_Debug::dump($_review->debug());
}
```

5. This code will give the same output, but the data of a collection is coming from objects and not directly from the database. The purpose of this is that we can directly call functions on the object.

 When working with Magento database tables, it is recommended to use the collections instead of a direct SQL query. More information about the Magento collection is described in the *Working with Magento collections* recipe from *Chapter 6, Databases and Modules*.

6. Print the URLs of the reviews on the screen. We can do this simply by calling the `getReviewUrl()` function on the `review` entities. Add the following code in each loop:

```
echo $_review->getReviewUrl().'<br/>';
```

7. While reloading the page, you will see that all the URLs of the reviews are printed. The logic of the URL structure is done in the `Mage_Review_Model_Review` class, which represents a `review` entity.

## How it works...

Working with flat tables in Magento is not so difficult. When using the Magento framework, a flat entity consists of the following parts:

▶ **The database table**: The database table is used to store the information of the entity. This database table can have relations to different tables in the Magento database, such as a relation with a product.

▶ **The model object**: The model object is a class where an instance is returned while loading a row from the database table. This class can have methods with business logic, such as the `getReviewUrl()` function in this recipe.

▶ **The resource model object**: The resource model is a class that connects the model with the database table. This class will handle, for example, the `save()` method.

▶ **The resource collection object**: The resource collection object is a class that makes it possible to work with Magento collections for an entity.

# Working with EAV tables

The EAV table is a database model that is used for some entities in Magento. In this recipe, we will explore the details of the EAV implementation in Magento.

## Getting ready

The EAV pattern is used for some entities in Magento such as the product entity. In this recipe, we will make some queries for updating a product using SQL queries. Open your database client and prepare yourself for running some complex queries.

## How to do it...

The following steps show you how you can create a query to return the data of a Magento EAV model:

1. The Magento EAV entities are declared in the `eav_entity_type` table. Run the following query to see which EAV entities are available:

   ```
   SELECT * FROM eav_entity_type;
   ```

   Remember the ID of the `catalog_product` entity.

2. To get the attributes related to a product, we have to look in the `eav_attribute` table. To see which attributes are related to a product, we have to run the following query:

   `SELECT * FROM eav_attribute WHERE entity_type_id = 10`

   Make sure `10` is the entity type ID for `catalog_product`.

3. Now we have the entity and attributes, so the value is the next part to find out. Find a product in the backend and remember the ID. For example, the product `HTC Touch Diamond` with the ID `166`.

4. Select the product from the `catalog_product_entity` table by running the following query:

   `SELECT * FROM catalog_product_entity WHERE entity_id = 166;`

5. The last query will only return the entity information of this product. To get the information for an attribute, such as `name`, we have to look in the `value` table. For the `name` attribute, the `value` table is `catalog_product_entity_varchar`. Run the following query to get all the `varchar` attribute values for the product:

   `SELECT * FROM catalog_product_entity_varchar WHERE entity_id = 166`

6. The previous query gives the following result:

| value_id Value ID | entity_type_id Entity Type ID | attribute_id Attribute ID | store_id Store ID | entity_id Entity ID | value Value |
|---|---|---|---|---|---|
| 1131 | 10 | 96 | 0 | 166 | HTC Touch Diamond |
| 1134 | 10 | 103 | 0 | 166 | |
| 1135 | 10 | 105 | 0 | 166 | |
| 1138 | 10 | 106 | 0 | 166 | /h/t/htc-touch-diamond.jpg |
| 1137 | 10 | 109 | 0 | 166 | /h/t/htc-touch-diamond.jpg |
| 1132 | 10 | 481 | 0 | 166 | htc-touch-diamond |
| 1136 | 10 | 493 | 0 | 166 | /h/t/htc-touch-diamond.jpg |
| 1133 | 10 | 562 | 0 | 166 | |
| 1517 | 10 | 570 | 0 | 166 | htc-touch-diamond |
| 1516 | 10 | 570 | 1 | 166 | htc-touch-diamond |
| 1139 | 10 | 571 | 0 | 166 | |
| 1140 | 10 | 836 | 0 | 166 | container2 |
| 1524 | 10 | 879 | 0 | 166 | NULL |
| 1523 | 10 | 880 | 0 | 166 | NULL |
| 1522 | 10 | 881 | 0 | 166 | NULL |
| 1521 | 10 | 931 | 0 | 166 | NULL |
| 1518 | 10 | 940 | 0 | 166 | NULL |
| 1519 | 10 | 941 | 0 | 166 | 2 |
| 1520 | 10 | 942 | 0 | 166 | 4 |

7. With this result, you can recognize the name of the product. If you look at the attribute ID of the row and match the attribute ID with the one in the `eav_attribute` table, you will see that this refers to the `name` attribute.

8. To update the name of the product, make an update query on the row as follows:

   ```
   UPDATE catalog_product_entity_varchar SET value = 'HTC Touch
   Diamond sql' WHERE value_id = 1131;
   ```

   See that the `value_id` value matches the value ID of your previous result.

9. Reload the product in the backend, and you will see that the name of the product is updated.

## How it works...

EAV entities in Magento are declared in the `eav_entity_type` table and the attributes are declared in the `eav_attribute` table.

Like every entity, each EAV entity has its own base table. In this base table, the primary fields are declared as columns in this table. All the other fields are declared as attributes in the `eav_attribute` table.

Every attribute is of a specific type such as `int`, `varchar`, `date`, `time`, `decimal`, and `text`. The place where these values are stored depends on the entity type and is declared in the configuration files of Magento.

The following screenshot shows the structure of the EAV tables for a product:

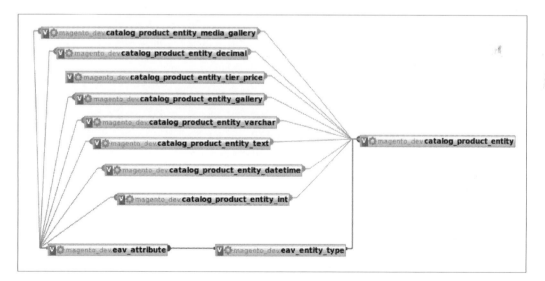

## There's more...

Not all EAV entities work with multiple tables by entity. For example, the `sales_flat_*` tables are all EAV tables, but they are, as their name suggests, flat. This means that all the attributes of the entity are set in a separate column of the flat table.

In the catalog configuration, you have the ability to enable the **Flat catalog** option for the tables for category and products. When this configuration is enabled, Magento will sync all the data from the EAV tables to the `catalog_flat_*` tables and will load the data from there.

When the **Flat catalog** option is enabled, you get a better performance because a `select` query on a single table is faster than getting the data from the different tables. The advantage is a better performance, but on the other hand, there are some disadvantages that could be a problem with a large amount of products and categories.

The Master data will be stored in the EAV tables. This means there is synchronization between the flat tables. This process is implemented as a **Magento Index Process**. When there are a lot of products and categories, this process can run very long. Another thing is that the size of the database can explode because the data is stored twice.

# Configuring a Master/Slave setup

**Database replication** is used when you want to scale your infrastructure to serve more requests. There are a lot of methods available to scale your database to set up replication. The exact choice is different for every situation.

In this recipe, we will use a generic setup to create a Master/Slave setup for our Magento store. This setup will use a Master database server where all the `write` queries will be saved. The Slave database server(s) will be used for the `read` queries. The database is the most difficult component of an application to scale.

## Getting ready

To complete the Master/Slave setup, we will use two different MySQL servers. Get the connection information such as hostname, IP addresses, username, and passwords.

## How to do it...

Here, we will set up a Master/Slave replication in MySQL and configure Magento to use this setup. Have a look at the following steps:

## Setting up the Master database

1. Log in to the server with SSH and open the `/etc/mysql/my.cnf` file.

2. Look for the `bind-address` section in the file and comment it out. By commenting this, you make it possible to make connections from different servers:

   ```
   #bind-address = 127.0.0.1
   ```

3. Paste the following code in the `my.cnf` file under the `[mysqld]` section:

   ```
   server-id = 1
   log_bin = /var/log/mysql/mysql-bin.log
   expire_logs_days = 10
   max_binlog_size = 100M
   binlog_do_db = magento_dev
   ```

4. Restart your MySQL server by running the following command:

   ```
   sudo service mysql restart
   ```

5. Open the MySQL shell by running the following command. This will perform a login with the root user:

   ```
   mysql -u root -p
   ```

6. When you are logged in, you have to run the following queries:

   ```
   GRANT ALL PRIVILEGES ON `magento_dev` . * TO `user_slave`@`%` WITH
   GRANT OPTION IDENTIFIED BY `password_slave`;
   FLUSH PRIVILEGES;
   ```

7. Run the following commands to show the status of the Master database:

   ```
   USE magento_dev;
   FLUSH TABLES WITH READ LOCK;
   SHOW MASTER STATUS;
   ```

   The last command from the previous snippet will give the following output:

   ```
   mysql> SHOW MASTER STATUS;
   +-------------------+----------+--------------+------------------+
   | File              | Position | Binlog_Do_DB | Binlog_Ignore_DB |
   +-------------------+----------+--------------+------------------+
   | mysql-bin.000001  |      369 | magentodb    |                  |
   +-------------------+----------+--------------+------------------+
   1 row in set (0.00 sec)
   ```

   We will use this information in the Slave setup, so keep this with you.

8. Unlock the tables with the following command:

```
UNLOCK TABLES;
quit;
```

While entering the `quit` or `exit` command, you will be returned to the shell of the server. The setup of the Master database is done.

## Setting up the Slave database

1. Perform an SSH login to your Slave server. This is a different server than your Master server.

2. Open the MySQL shell with the following command:

```
mysql -u root -p
```

3. Create a new database `magento_dev` and import the Master database in it.

4. Add the following configuration in the `/etc/mysql/my.cnf` file under the [mysqld] section:

```
[mysqld]
server-id = 2
master-host = 192.168.56.3
master-user = user_slave
master-password = password_slave
master-connect-retry = 60
replicate-do-db = magento_dev
```

5. Restart the MySQL server with the following command:

```
sudo service mysql restart
```

6. Run the following commands in your MySQL shell. Make sure the MASTER_LOG_FILE and MASTER_LOG_POST values match the values that you have seen while running the SHOW MASTER STATUS command:

```
CHANGE MASTER TO MASTER_HOST=`192.168.56.3`, MASTER_USER=`user_
slave`, MASTER_PASSWORD=`password_slave`, MASTER_LOG_FILE=`mysql-
bin.000001`, MASTER_LOG_POS=88;
```

7. Run the following command to start the Slave server:

```
START SLAVE;
```

8. Check the status by running the following command:

```
SHOW SLAVE STATUS \G
```

The output will look as follows:

```
mysql> SHOW SLAVE STATUS \G
*************************** 1. row ***************************
               Slave_IO_State:
                  Master_Host: 192.168.55.3
                  Master_User: root
                  Master_Port: 3306
                Connect_Retry: 60
              Master_Log_File: mysql-bin.000002
          Read_Master_Log_Pos: 107
               Relay_Log_File: mysqld-relay-bin.000001
                Relay_Log_Pos: 4
        Relay_Master_Log_File: mysql-bin.000002
             Slave_IO_Running: No
            Slave_SQL_Running: Yes
              Replicate_Do_DB:
          Replicate_Ignore_DB:
           Replicate_Do_Table:
       Replicate_Ignore_Table:
      Replicate_Wild_Do_Table:
  Replicate_Wild_Ignore_Table:
                   Last_Errno: 0
                   Last_Error:
                 Skip_Counter: 0
          Exec_Master_Log_Pos: 107
              Relay_Log_Space: 107
              Until_Condition: None
               Until_Log_File:
                Until_Log_Pos: 0
            Master_SSL_Allowed: No
            Master_SSL_CA_File:
            Master_SSL_CA_Path:
               Master_SSL_Cert:
             Master_SSL_Cipher:
                Master_SSL_Key:
         Seconds_Behind_Master: NULL
Master_SSL_Verify_Server_Cert: No
                Last_IO_Errno: 0
                Last_IO_Error:
               Last_SQL_Errno: 0
               Last_SQL_Error:
   Replicate_Ignore_Server_Ids:
              Master_Server_Id: 2
1 row in set (0.00 sec)

mysql>
```

## Configuring Magento

Now, when the MySQL setup for the Master/Slave setup is done, it is time to configure Magento to use this setup. We have to configure this in the app/etc/local.xml file of Magento. Here, we will configure a default_setup connection and a default_read connection. To configure this, add the following XML in the local.xml file under the <resources> tag:

```
<resources>
    <db>
        <table_prefix><![CDATA[]]></table_prefix>
    </db>
    <default_setup>
        <connection>
```

```
            <host><![CDATA[192.168.56.3]]></host>
            <username><![CDATA[user_master]]></username>
            <password><![CDATA[password_master]]></password>
            <dbname><![CDATA[magento_dev]]></dbname>
            <initStatements><![CDATA[SET NAMES utf8]]>
            </initStatements>
            <model><![CDATA[mysql4]]></model>
            <type><![CDATA[pdo_mysql]]></type>
            <pdoType><![CDATA[]]></pdoType>
            <active>1</active>
        </connection>
    </default_setup>
    <default_read>
        <connection>
            <host><![CDATA[192.168.56.3]]></host>
            <username><![CDATA[user_slave]]></username>
            <password><![CDATA[password_slave]]></password>
            <dbname><![CDATA[magento_dev]]></dbname>
            <active>1</active>
        </connection>
    </default_read>
</resources>
```

Clear your cache and your Magento will use this setup.

## How it works...

When data in the Master database changes, it has to be in sync with the Slave database. To establish this, the binary logfile is used to communicate between each other.

You have to see that binary logging is configured on the Master. If not, you have to enable this and restart your MySQL server. If it is not enabled, there is no logfile, so there is no communication between servers. This is also the reason why the MASTER_LOG_FILE Slave must match the one on the Master database.

If the setup is done and the Magento configuration is in the app/etc/local.xml file, everything is finished. Magento is smart enough to send the write request to the Master and the read requests to the Slave.

# Repairing the database

Sometimes it happens that your Magento database is broken or corrupt. This can be caused by various reasons such as hacking or server crash. When the database is broken and you have to fix it, the database repair tool from Magento is of great help.

In this recipe, we will make our database corrupt and fix it with the repair tool.

## Getting ready

To prepare you, download the **database repair tool** from the Magento site at `http://www.magentocommerce.com` and place the PHP file in your server root.

## How to do it...

The following steps show you how to make your database corrupt and fix it using the database repair tool:

1. Create a backup of your existing database.
2. Create an empty database as the reference database. Let's say we call it `magento_dev_repair`.
3. Configure Magento to use this database in the `app/etc/local.xml` file.
4. Clear the cache and run Magento. This will install an empty Magento in this database.
5. Make your original database corrupt. You can do this by running the following queries that remove a foreign key and a table:

   ```
   ALTER TABLE core_store DROP FOREIGN KEY FK_CORE_STORE_GROUP_ID_
   CORE_STORE_GROUP_GROUP_ID;
   ```

   ```
   DROP TABLE catalog_product_index_price
   ```

6. Browse to the repair tool in your browser, and configure your original and reference database as shown in the following screenshot:

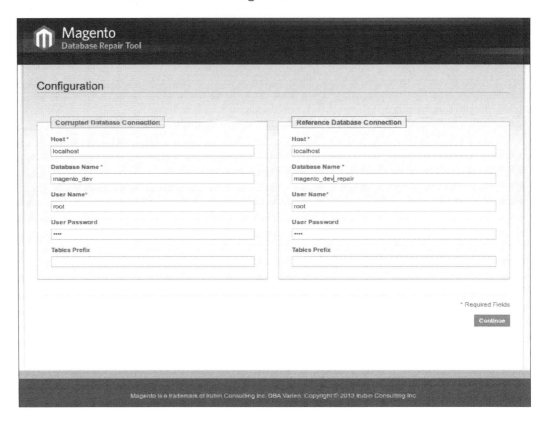

7. Submit the form and the script will repair your database. On the next page, you will see what changes are made to your original database.

8. Switch the database in the `app/etc/local.xml` file, so Magento uses your original database.

9. Clear the cache and your shop is up and running.

## How it works...

While running the database repair tool, the script will compare the original database with the reference database. If the comparison is done, the script will make the structure of your original database the same as the one of the reference databases.

The database repair tool only fixes structural issues with your database. If you miss some data, this is not the right tool to get the data back.

# 6
# Databases and Modules

In this chapter, we will cover:

- ▶ Registering the resource models
- ▶ Registering connections
- ▶ Installing and upgrading scripts
- ▶ Creating a flat table with models
- ▶ Working with Magento collections

## Introduction

In the previous chapter, we learned how the Magento database works, which connections are available, and how we can interact with the database.

In this chapter, we will perform some practical tasks with the things we learned in the previous chapter. We will extend the module that we created in *Chapter 4, Creating a Module*, with database interactions.

We will create Magento models that will interact with a database table, which will be installed by the module.

## Registering the resource models

The first thing we have to do is to register the **resource** models. The normal models are used to write business logic. The resource models are used to interact with the database.

## Getting ready

We have to add an extra configuration in the `config.xml` file of the module. Open the `app/code/local/Packt/Helloworld/etc/config.xml` file.

## How to do it...

The following steps explain how to register resource models in the existing `Packt_Helloworld` module:

1.  Navigate to the tag where the models are registered. This is in the `config/global/models` tag.

2.  Add the following configuration in it to add the resource models. Your `<global>` tag will look as follows:

```xml
<global>
    <blocks>
        <helloworld>
            <class>Packt_Helloworld_Block</class>
        </helloworld>
    </blocks>
    <helpers>
        <helloworld>
            <class>Packt_Helloworld_Helper</class>
        </helloworld>
    </helpers>
    <models>
        <helloworld>
            <class>Packt_Helloworld_Model</class>
        </helloworld>
        <helloworld_resource>
            <class>Packt_Helloworld_Model_Resource</class>
        </helloworld_resource>
    </models>
</global>
```

3.  Create the `app/code/local/Packt/Helloworld/Model/Resource` folder.

4.  Link the normal model with the resource model by adding the following XML code in the `<models>` tag. The `<models>` tag will look as follows:

```xml
<models>
    <helloworld>
        <class>Packt_Helloworld_Model</class>
        <resourceModel>helloworld_resource</resourceModel>
    </helloworld>
```

```
<helloworld_resource>
    <class>Packt_Helloworld_Model_Resource</class>
</helloworld_resource>
</models>
```

The link between the `helloworld` and `helloworld_resource` models is done with the `<resourceModel>` tag.

5. Test your configuration with the `wiz` command-line tool by running the following command:

```
wiz devel-models | grep helloworld
```

You will now get the following output:

```
$ wiz devel-models | grep helloworld
| helloworld/*              | Packt_Helloworld_Model_*           |
| helloworld_resource/*     | Packt_Helloworld_Model_Resource_*  |
$
```

The previous command will display all registered models and filter the output on rows matching the `helloworld` word.

## How it works...

The models in Magento are used for business logic. For example, an observer model usually contains functions that will be triggered by events or cron jobs.

A Magento object can also represent an entity such as a product, customer, and category. The models representing an entity usually inherit from the `Mage_Core_Model_Abstract` class. This class has logic to connect with a resource model. For example, the `save()` function is declared in this class.

When you look in the `save()` function of the `Mage_Core_Model_Abstract` class, you see that the `getResource()` function is called. This `getResource()` function will return an instance of the resource model.

Resource models are used to connect entities with the database. Magento-specific business logic is written in the model and the model is called while working with an entity.

If you want to get a resource model instance, you can use the `Mage::getResourceModel()` or `Mage::getResourceSingleton()` method. To get an instance of a class, we have to pass the Magento classname as the first argument.

# Registering connections

In this recipe, we will configure the `read` and `write` adapters to use it in this module. These adapters are used to connect the models with the database.

## Getting ready

We will add the adapter configuration in the `config.xml` file of the `Packt_Helloworld` module. Open this file and get ready to add some configuration.

## How to do it...

Follow the next steps to create the `read` and `write` connections of the `Packt_Helloworld` module:

1. Navigate to the `<global>` tag and add the following configuration to it. This will register the `read` adapter.

   ```
   <resources>
       <helloworld_read>
           <connection>
               <use>core_read</use>
           </connection>
       </helloworld_read>
   </resources>
   ```

2. Configure the `write` adapter to add the following in the `<resources>` tag of the XML code. Your resources tag will look as follows:

   ```
   <resources>
       <helloworld_write>
           <connection>
               <use>core_write</use>
           </connection>
       </helloworld_write>
       <helloworld_read>
           <connection>
               <use>core_read</use>
           </connection>
       </helloworld_read>
   </resources>
   ```

3. Clear your cache and you're done.

## How it works...

Every model in Magento is associated with a `read` and `write` adapter. The default `read` adapter is `core_read`. The default `write` adapter is `core_write`.

Normally, all models use the `core_read` and `core_write` adapters when the database tables are in the Magento database.

## There's more...

You can register and configure a specific database model that uses another database connection. If you navigate to the following URL, you can find a good tutorial that explains this:

```
http://www.solvingmagento.com/accessing-an-external-database-from-
your-magento-module/
```

# Installing and upgrading scripts

When your module uses a custom database table, you need to make certain changes to the database to deploy your module on a staging or production server. Magento has a way to automatically trigger and install or update scripts when the code is in the right place.

In this recipe, we will extend the `Packt_Helloworld` module with the `install` script. This `install` script will add an attribute to all products.

## Getting ready

For this recipe, we have to work in the module's folder and the database. Open your database client and go to your code in the `Packt_Helloworld` module.

## How to do it...

The following steps describe the procedure to create and install scripts for your module:

1.  Initialize the setup procedures for the module by adding the following code in the `<resources>` tag of the `config.xml` file:

```
<helloworld_setup>
    <setup>
        <module>Packt_Helloworld</module>
        <class>Mage_Eav_Model_Entity_Setup</class>
    </setup>
    <connection>
```

```
        <use>core_setup</use>
    </connection>
</helloworld_setup>
```

The previous code will initialize a setup procedure with the name `helloworld_setup`. The `<module>` tag configures the relation with the `Packt_Helloworld` module.

2. Create the folder for the installation scripts. The folder name in this case is `app/code/local/Packt/Helloworld/sql/helloworld_setup`.

3. Create the installation script. The naming of an installation script follows the convention `install-<version_number_config_xml>.php`. In our case, the name of this script is `install-0.0.1.php`.

4. Add the following content in the file to test the installation procedure:

```
die('test');
```

5. Clear the cache and reload any page from the frontend. You will see a white page with **Test** on it.

>  An installation or upgrade script is made to run once during an installation. The version number of every registered setup is stored in the `core_resource` database table. When you want to run your script again for testing it, you can remove an entry or change the version number for a setup.

6. Add the following content in the installation script. This installs a product attribute that is available for all products.

```php
<?php

$installer = $this;

$installer->startSetup();

$installer->addAttribute('catalog_product', 'helloworld_label',
array(
            'group'         => 'Helloworld',
            'type'          => 'varchar',
            'label'         => 'Helloworld label',
            'input'         => 'text',
            'global'        => Mage_Catalog_Model_Resource_Eav_
                               Attribute::SCOPE_STORE,
            'visible'       => true,
            'required'      => false,
```

```
'searchable'          => false,
'filterable'          => false,
'comparable'          => false,
'visible_on_front'    => true,
'unique'              => false,
'apply_to'            => 'simple,configurable,virtual,
                         bundle,downloadable',
'is_configurable'     => false
));
```

`$installer->endSetup();`

The previous code will create the `helloworld_label` product attribute. The attribute will be applied to all products.

With the `group` option, the attribute will be displayed in the **Helloworld** tab while viewing a product in the backend.

7. Clear the cache and reload the page. While reloading a page after clearing cache, the installation script will run automatically.

8. Go to the backend and open a product to check whether the product attribute is added. Normally, you will see a **Helloworld** tab with the attribute in it similar to the following screenshot:

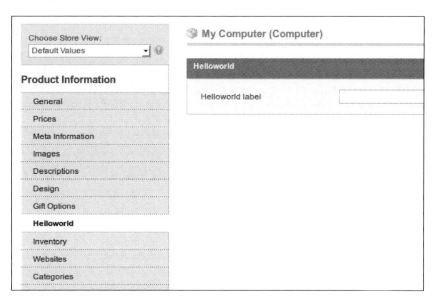

9. When your installation script is executed, you can see your setup in the `core_resource` table of Magento. In this table, all modules and version numbers are stored, so Magento knows which installation or upgradation scripts have to be executed.

## How it works...

Working with installation scripts is useful when you want to change something in the structure of your database. Some of the purposes are:

- Easy deployment of your site from your development/test environment to your production environment
- Ability to repair the database
- Overview of the database changes

The `$this` object in the installation scripts is the class we have declared in the setup registration in the `config.xml` file. In this case, it is the `Mage_Eav_Model_Entity_Setup` class. This class is mostly used when you want to add EAV attributes to the entities such as a product or category like we did in this recipe. Mostly all setup classes extend the default setup class, that is, `Mage_Core_Model_Resource_Setup`.

If you want to do a lot of things in you installation script, you can create your own setup class. This will extend from the normal setup classes.

The functions declared in this class can call the `$this` object in the installer file.

# Creating a flat table with models

In this recipe, we will extend our module with a flat database table. We will create an upgradation script with the instruction to create a table. When the table is created, we will finish the setup by adding the needed Magento models, resource models, and collections. After finishing the whole setup, we have created a custom Magento entity with all the features of the Magento ORM.

## Getting ready

For this recipe, we have to work with the code and the database. Open your IDE in the `module` folder and get access to your database client.

## How to do it...

The following steps are the instructions to create a database table with the appropriate Magento models that can interact with this table:

1. Configure the table name in the `app/code/local/Packt/Helloworld/etc/config.xml` file.

2. Add the following code under the `helloworld_resource` tag so that the tag looks as follows:

```
<helloworld_resource>
    <class>Packt_Helloworld_Model_Resource</class>
    <entities>
        <subscription>
            <table>helloworld_subscription</table>
        </subscription>
    </entities>
</helloworld_resource>
```

The previous code will declare an entity which references the `helloworld_subscription` table.

3. Create the upgradation script by creating the `app/code/local/Packt/Helloworld/sql/helloworld_setup/upgrade-0.0.1-0.0.2.php` file.

4. Add the following code in the upgradation file. This code is a command to create a table with some fields.

```php
<?php

$installer = $this;

$installer->startSetup();

$table = $installer->getConnection()
    ->newTable($installer->getTable('helloworld/subscription'))
    ->addColumn('subscription_id', Varien_Db_Ddl_Table::
    TYPE_INTEGER, null, array(
        'identity'  => true,
        'unsigned'  => true,
        'nullable'  => false,
        'primary'   => true,
        ), 'Subscription id')
    ->addColumn('created_at', Varien_Db_Ddl_Table::
    TYPE_TIMESTAMP, null, array(
        'nullable'  => false,
        ), 'Created at')
    ->addColumn('updated_at', Varien_Db_Ddl_Table::
    TYPE_TIMESTAMP, null, array(
        'nullable'  => false,
        ), 'Updated at')
```

```
                ->addColumn('firstname', Varien_Db_Ddl_Table::TYPE_TEXT,
                64, array(
                        'nullable'    => false,
                        ), 'First name')
                ->addColumn('lastname', Varien_Db_Ddl_Table::TYPE_TEXT,
                64, array(
                        'nullable'    => false,
                        ), 'Last name')
                ->addColumn('email', Varien_Db_Ddl_Table::TYPE_TEXT,
                64, array(
                        'nullable'    => false,
                        ), 'Email address')
                ->addColumn('status', Varien_Db_Ddl_Table::TYPE_TEXT,
                32, array(
                        'nullable'    => false,
                        'default'     => 'pending',
                        ), 'Status')
                ->addColumn('message', Varien_Db_Ddl_Table::TYPE_TEXT,
                '64k', array(
                        'unsigned'    => true,
                        'nullable'    => false,
                        ), 'Subscription notes')
                ->addIndex($installer->getIdxName('helloworld/subscription',
                array('email')),
                        array('email'))
                ->setComment('Helloworld subscriptions');
        $installer->getConnection()->createTable($table);

        $installer->endSetup();
```

5. Clear the cache and reload the frontend. When you refresh your tables in the database client, you will see the `helloworld_subscription` table in the list.

While creating a table, think about the naming convention. The first part is the name where the models are registered followed by an underscore. The second part refers to the entity model.

Make sure the name of the model is singular. For this example, it is `subscription` and not `subscriptions`.

6. Check whether the table is installed in the database. Reload the tables in phpMyAdmin and open the new table. The structure will look as follows:

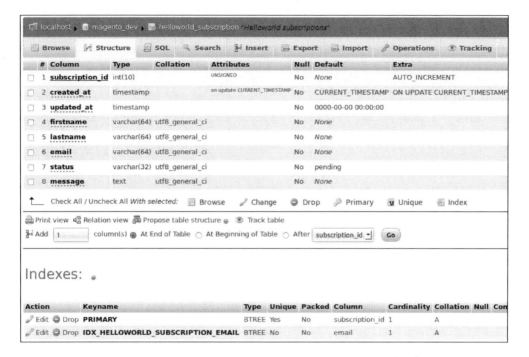

7. When the table is installed with the upgradation script (from 0.0.1 to 0.0.2), the last part is to create a Magento entity that communicates with the previously created table. For doing this, we have to create a model, a resource model, and a collection resource model. The first step is to create the following files:

   ❑ `app/code/local/Packt/Helloworld/Model/Subscription.php` (the model)

   ❑ `app/code/local/Packt/Helloworld/Model/Resource/Subscription.php` (the resource model)

   ❑ `app/code/local/Packt/Helloworld/Model/Resource/Subscription/Collection.php` (the resource collection model)

8. Open the model file and add the following content to it. This content will link the model with the appropriate resource model.

```php
<?php
class Packt_Helloworld_Model_Subscription extends Mage_Core_Model_
Abstract
{
```

```
        protected function _construct()
        {
            $this->_init('helloworld/subscription');
        }

    }
```

9. Open the resource model file and add the following content to it. The next content will link the model with the database. In the _init function, we will link the model with the primary key of the database table.

```php
<?php
class Packt_Helloworld_Model_Resource_Subscription extends Mage_
Core_Model_Resource_Db_Abstract
{

    protected function _construct() {
        $this->_init('helloworld/subscription',
        'subscription_id');
    }

}
```

10. Open the resource collection model file and add the following content to it. This file makes it possible to work with Magento collections on the model when you call the getCollection() method on an entity.

```php
<?php
class Packt_Helloworld_Model_Resource_Subscription_Collection
extends Mage_Core_Model_Resource_Db_Collection_Abstract
{

    protected function _construct() {
        $this->_init('helloworld/subscription');
    }

}
```

11. All the files are at the right place to start the tests if everything went well so far. To perform some tests, create a subscriptionAction() method in the IndexController of the module where we can perform some tests.

12. Navigate to the new action in the controller by going to the http://magento-dev. local/helloworld/index/subscription URL. You will see a blank page.

13. Add the following content in the action that will create a new subscription item in our table:

```
public function subscriptionAction()
{
    $subscription = Mage::getModel('helloworld/subscription');

    $subscription->setFirstname('John');
    $subscription->setLastname('Doe');
    $subscription->setEmail('john.doe@example.com');
    $subscription->setMessage('A short message to test');

    $subscription->save();

    echo 'success';
}
```

14. When you reload the page, you will see the word **success**. This word being displayed is a sign that all the actions have successfully executed. Navigate to your database and make the following query:

    **SELECT * FROM helloworld_subscription;**

    This query will give you the following output:

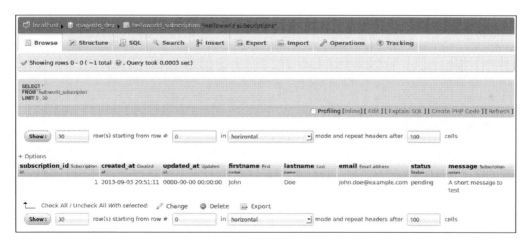

## How it works...

When you work with the previous setup for entities in a database table, the Magento ORM makes the link between the entity and the database.

In our previously created Magento entity (`Mage::getModel('helloworld/subscription')`), we can use the following functions that will result in a query to the database:

- `load($entityId)`
- `save()`
- `delete()`

All these functions are implemented in the `Mage_Core_Model_Abstract` class. All the Magento entities will extend this abstract class to use the ORM framework.

# Working with Magento collections

In this chapter, we will explore the possibilities of the Magento collections. A Magento collection is a set of **entities** where you can add filters to customize your result.

In this chapter, we will explore everything that is possible with Magento collections.

## Getting ready

Go to the `indexController` of the `helloworld` module and create a `collectionAction` method in it. In this action, we will perform some tests to compare the results.

## How to do it...

The next examples show what are the possibilities while working with Magento collections:

1.  Add the following code in the `collectionAction` method and navigate to the page. This code will return 10 products.

    ```
    public function collectionAction ()
    {

        $productCollection = Mage::getModel('catalog/product')
                ->getCollection()
                ->setPageSize(10,1);
    ```

```
foreach ($productCollection as $product)
{
    Zend_Debug::dump($product->debug());
}

}
```

 At the end of the code, there is a `foreach` loop. This calls the `debug()` function on the object. The `debug()` function is available on all objects that extend the `Varien_Object` function. A collection dump is a very large array and can cause an **out of memory** exception in PHP or very large responses in the browser.

2. When you look at the output, you will see the following array:

```
array(11) {
  ["entity_id"] => string(2) "16"
  ["entity_type_id"] => string(2) "10"
  ["attribute_set_id"] => string(2) "38"
  ["type_id"] => string(6) "simple"
  ["sku"] => string(5) "n2610"
  ["created_at"] => string(19) "2007-08-23 13:03:05"
  ["updated_at"] => string(19) "2008-08-08 14:50:04"
  ["has_options"] => string(1) "0"
  ["required_options"] => string(1) "0"
  ["is_salable"] => string(1) "1"
  ["stock_item (Varien_Object)"] => array(1) {
    ["is_in_stock"] => string(1) "1"
  }
}
```

3. The values in this object don't contain attribute values. To select them, we have to use the `addAttributeToSelect('<attribute_code>')` function. Add the following code to select the first 10 products with the name, price, and image attributes:

```
public function collectionAction ()
{

    $productCollection = Mage::getModel('catalog/product')
            ->getCollection()
            ->addAttributeToSelect('name')
            ->addAttributeToSelect('price')
            ->addAttributeToSelect('image')
```

```
            ->setPageSize(10,1);

    foreach ($productCollection as $product)
    {
        Zend_Debug::dump($product->debug());
    }

}
```

This code will output an array for each product as shown in the following code:

```
array(14) {
  ["entity_id"] => string(2) "16"
  ["entity_type_id"] => string(2) "10"
  ["attribute_set_id"] => string(2) "38"
  ["type_id"] => string(6) "simple"
  ["sku"] => string(5) "n2610"
  ["created_at"] => string(19) "2007-08-23 13:03:05"
  ["updated_at"] => string(19) "2008-08-08 14:50:04"
  ["has_options"] => string(1) "0"
  ["required_options"] => string(1) "0"
  ["name"] => string(16) "Nokia 2610 Phone"
  ["image"] => string(27) "/n/o/nokia-2610-phone-2.jpg"
  ["price"] => string(8) "149.9900"
  ["is_salable"] => string(1) "1"
  ["stock_item (Varien_Object)"] => array(1) {
    ["is_in_stock"] => string(1) "1"
  }
}
```

4. We will now create a filter on the product collection. The next code shows how you can filter the products with the name **Nokia 2610 Phone**:

```
public function collectionAction ()
{

    $productCollection = Mage::getModel('catalog/product')
            ->getCollection()
            ->addAttributeToSelect('price')
            ->addAttributeToSelect('image')
            ->addAttributeToFilter('name', 'Nokia 2610 Phone');

    foreach ($productCollection as $_product)
    {
        Zend_Debug::dump($_product->debug());
    }

}
```

The code in this statement will create a WHERE name = 'Nokia 2610 Phone' statement to the query, so all the items with the name **Nokia 2610 Phone** will be returned.

5. With the addAttributeToFilter function, we can do more. The following code shows how you can create a WHERE product_id IN (159, 160, 161) statement:

```
public function collectionAction ()
{

    $productCollection = Mage::getModel('catalog/product')
            ->getCollection()
            ->addAttributeToSelect('price')
            ->addAttributeToSelect('image')
            ->addAttributeToFilter('entity_id', array(
                'in' => array(159, 160, 161)
            ));

    foreach ($productCollection as $_product)
    {
        Zend_Debug::dump($_product->debug());
    }

}
```

6. The next filter we will use is the like filter. Add the following code to make a query with the WHERE name LIKE '%PC%' statement:

```
public function collectionAction ()
{

    $productCollection = Mage::getModel('catalog/product')
            ->getCollection()
            ->addAttributeToSelect('price')
            ->addAttributeToSelect('image')
            ->addAttributeToFilter('name', array(
                'like' => '%PC%'
            ));

    foreach ($productCollection as $_product)
    {
        Zend_Debug::dump($_product->debug());
    }

}
```

7. When the queries get more complex, sometimes it is nice to know what SQL query will be generated to get the collection. To print the SQL query, which is used for a collection, we can use the following line of code:

```
$productCollection->getSelect()->__toString()
```

8. When you add the following code, you will see the query for this collection:

```
public function collectionAction ()
{

        $productCollection = Mage::getModel('catalog/product')
                ->getCollection()
                ->addAttributeToSelect('price')
                ->addAttributeToSelect('image')
                ->addAttributeToFilter('name', array(
                    'like' => '%PC%'
                ));

        $productCollection->load();

        echo $productCollection->getSelect()->__toString();

}
```

This code will output the following SQL query:

```
SELECT `e`.*,
        IF(at_name.value_id > 0, at_name.value,
        at_name_default.value) AS `name`,
        `price_index`.`price`,
        `price_index`.`tax_class_id`,
        `price_index`.`final_price`,
        IF(price_index.tier_price IS NOT NULL,
        Least(price_index.min_price,
                                        price_index.tier_price),
        price_index.min_price)
AS
        `minimal_price`,
        `price_index`.`min_price`,
        `price_index`.`max_price`,
        `price_index`.`tier_price`
```

```
FROM      `catalog_product_entity` AS `e`
          INNER JOIN `catalog_product_entity_varchar` AS
          `at_name_default`
                  ON ( `at_name_default`.`entity_id` =
                  `e`.`entity_id` )
                     AND ( `at_name_default`.`attribute_id` = '96' )
                     AND `at_name_default`.`store_id` = 0
                     LEFT JOIN `catalog_product_entity_varchar`
                        AS `at_name`
                ON ( `at_name`.`entity_id` = `e`.`entity_id` )
                    AND ( `at_name`.`attribute_id` = '96' )
                    AND ( `at_name`.`store_id` = 1 )
                    INNER JOIN `catalog_product_index_price`
                       AS `price_index`
                ON price_index.entity_id = e.entity_id
                    AND price_index.website_id = '1'
                    AND price_index.customer_group_id = 0
WHERE     ( IF(at_name.value_id > 0, at_name.value, at_name_default.
value) LIKE
              '%PC%' )
```

 When using the `getSelect()->__toString()` function, make sure the collection is loaded. This is why we called the `$productCollection->load()` function before printing the SQL statement. When you add a collection in a `foreach()` loop, the collection will automatically be loaded.

Run this query in phpMyAdmin, and you will see that this flat response can be used to create a product collection.

9. With the previous code examples, we can only read data from the database. By using the `setDataToAll()` function, you can update some attributes for all the entities in the collection. Use the next code to update all the prices in the collection:

```
public function collectionAction ()
{

    $productCollection = Mage::getModel('catalog/product')
            ->getCollection()
            ->addAttributeToSelect('price')
            ->addAttributeToSelect('image')
```

```
            ->addAttributeToFilter('name', array(
                'like' => '%PC%'
            ));

    $productCollection->setDataToAll('price', 20);

    foreach ($productCollection as $_product)
    {
        Zend_Debug::dump($_product->debug());
    }

}
```

10. When you use the `setDataToAll()` function, nothing will be changed in the database until you have called the `save()` function. Add the following code after the `setDataToAll()` function to save the collection:

```
$productCollection->save();
```

## How it works...

When you want to get a collection of entities, you can do this by calling the next two methods. The return value of these two is a collection object.

```
Mage::getModel('model/entity')->getCollection();
Mage::getResourceModel('model/entity_collection');
```

A Magento collection object always extends from the `Varien_Data_Collection` class. This object works as an array, so you can iterate between items in a collection.

For every entity, a collection class is created in the resource model folder. In most cases, this class extends the parent classes and in some cases, methods are added specially for an entity.

The product entity is a good example of this. When you open the `Mage_Catalog_Model_Resource_Product_Collection` class, you will see that this class is not empty. Here, some functions are declared specially for the product entity.

When you debug the inheritance of collections, you will see that there is a difference for flat and EAV entities as you can see in the following diagram:

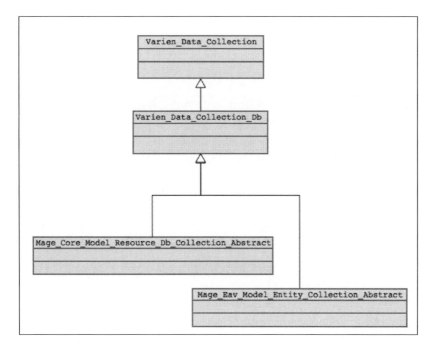

You can see that the classes of the flat entities (`Mage_Core_Model_Resource_Db_ Collection_Abstract`) and EAV entities (`Mage_Eav_Model_Entity_Collection_ Abstract`) extend the same parents. The EAV class adds extra methods and redefines some existing ones to work together with the EAV system.

This is the main reason why the collection queries are different for flat and EAV entities.

For adding a filter on a field, the function for EAV is `addAttributeToFilter()`. For a flat entity, the function is `addFieldToFilter()`. The `addAttributeToFilter()` function is declared in the `Mage_Eav_Model_Entity_Collection_Abstract` class, so it is not available in the `Varien_Data_Collection_Db` class.

## See also

If you want to know all the possibilities on offer for Magento collections, have a look at the following article on the Magento website, which has information on all the functions and options:

```
http://www.magentocommerce.com/wiki/1_-_installation_and_
configuration/using_collections_in_magento
```

# 7

# Magento Backend

In this chapter, we will cover the following topics:

- ▶ Registering a backend controller
- ▶ Extending the menu
- ▶ Adding an ACL
- ▶ Extending the system configuration
- ▶ Creating a grid from a database table
- ▶ Adding customer attributes
- ▶ Working with source models

## Introduction

For a store owner, the backend is the interface to manage everything in their store. It is very important that everything is secured against visitors with bad intentions. The backend of a standard Magento installation is extendible in many ways, so everyone can extend it with custom pages, configuration, roles, and more.

By following the configuration patterns of Magento, all the security issues (access for anonymous users, a secured environment, and so on) are covered by the backend system of Magento. The recipes in this chapter describe all the ways in which you can extend your backend using Magento's best practices of extending the backend.

## Registering a backend controller

The first thing that we will learn is how to extend the backend with a custom controller action. For this, we have to create a controller that is secured so that only logged-in backend users can see the content of this page.

You need a backend controller when you want to add an extra page to your backend. This is mostly the case when you are working with a custom form or overview that you need for your module.

## Getting ready

To make the testing of the admin URLs easier, we will remove the secret key (the hash in the URL of a backend page) from the admin URLs. You can configure this in **System | Configuration | Admin | Security**. Change the configuration as shown in the following screenshot:

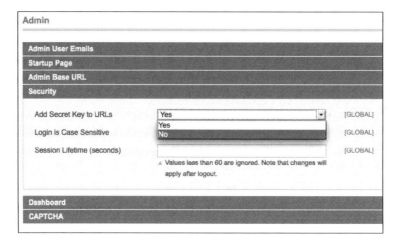

## How to do it...

When you want to add an extra page to your backend, you have to perform the following steps:

1.  Open the `app/code/local/Packt/Helloworld/etc/config.xml` file and add the following configuration under the `global` tag:

```
<admin>
  <routers>
    <adminhtml>
      <args>
        <modules>
          <helloworld before="Mage_Adminhtml">Packt_Helloworld_
          Adminhtml
          </helloworld>
        </modules>
      </args>
    </adminhtml>
  </routers>
</admin>
```

This configuration will initialize the `Adminhtml` module to look for controllers in the folders of the `Packt_Helloworld` module.

2. Add the following folders in the directories as shown:

   ❑ `app/code/local/Packt/Helloworld/controllers/Adminhtml`

   ❑ `app/code/local/Packt/Helloworld/controllers/Adminhtml/Helloworld`

3. In the last folder, create the `IndexController.php` file with the following content:

```php
<?php
class Packt_Helloworld_Adminhtml_Helloworld_IndexController
extends Mage_Adminhtml_Controller_Action
{
  public function indexAction()
  {

  }
}
```

4. Make sure that you extend from the `Mage_Adminhtml_Controller_Action` class so that all the security cases are covered.

5. Clear the cache and navigate to the controller by going to the URL `http://magento-dev.local/index.php/admin/helloworld_index/`.

   This will give you a white page. This is normal because the action is empty.

6. Add the following code in your `indexAction` function and reload the page. You will see that an empty backend page is returned:

```php
$this->loadLayout();
$this->renderLayout();
```

## How it works...

The difference between a frontend and backend controller is the parent class. A backend controller extends another class as the frontend controller. A backend controller always extends from the `Mage_Adminhtml_Controller_Action` class. This class adds the security to the controller so that only authenticated users can have access to the controller action(s).

When we add the configuration in the `config.xml` file, we will extend the `controllers` folder of the `Mage_Adminhtml` module with the `controllers/Adminhtml` folder of our module. With the `before="Mage_Adminhtml"` option, Magento will look for a controller file in the folder of the module. Later, it will look in the `Mage_Adminhtml` module.

When you create a backend controller for your module, make sure that you add the `Adminhtml/Modulename` folder in the `controllers` folder to avoid conflicts with the existing `Mage_Adminhtml` controllers.

## There's more...

In some modules and tutorials, you will find the following configuration to link your backend controller:

```
<admin>
  <routers>
    <helloworld>
      <use>admin</use>
      <args>
        <module>Packt_Helloworld</module>
        <frontName>helloworld</frontName>
      </args>
    </helloworld>
  </routers>
</admin>
```

It is *not* recommended to do the configuration in this way because this will create issues when you work with frontend and backend controllers in the same module.

# Extending the menu

While extending the backend, it is important to make sure that the user can easily navigate to your customized pages. The only alternative that you can use for this is to extend the **Admin** menu with your own items. With the Magento framework, it is possible to add menu items at every level in that menu.

## Getting ready

For this recipe, the only task that we have to do is add the right configuration, which is in the `adminhtml.xml` file, into the `etc` folder of the `Packt_Helloworld` module.

## How to do it...

The following steps describe how you can add an extra menu item to the **Admin** menu:

1. The first thing that we have to think about is where will we place an extra menu item in the **Admin** menu. For this test, we will place it under the **System** menu. Keep the system ID in mind. We have to use this for the menu configuration.

2. The second thing is to add the configuration in the `adminhtml.xml` file. Paste the following code under the `config` tag:

```
<menu>
  <system>
    <children>
      <helloworld translate="title" module="helloworld">
        <title>Helloworld</title>
        <sort_order>10</sort_order>
        <action>adminhtml/helloworld_index</action>
      </helloworld>
    </children>
  </system>
</menu>
```

 In the `<helloworld>` tag, you see the `translate` and `module` attributes. When these attributes are set, the title will be translated using the helper class of the `helloworld` module.

3. Clear the cache and reload the backend. While hovering over the system menu, you will see that a **Helloworld** link is displayed as shown the following screenshot:

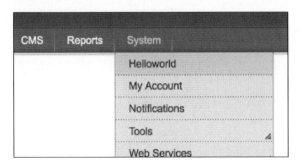

4. To change the position of the menu item, we have to add the following `sort_order` tag in the configuration:

```
<sort_order>30</sort_order>
```

## How it works...

The **Admin** menu of Magento comprises all menu configuration data from the modules. The standard menu contains the following 10 root items:

- ▶  Dashboard
- ▶  Sales
- ▶  Catalog
- ▶  Mobile
- ▶  Customers
- ▶  Promotions
- ▶  Newsletter
- ▶  Reports
- ▶  System

When you want to add an item as a child of one of the root items, you have to use these tags in your configuration as we did for this recipe. The IDs of these menu items are declared in the configuration XML files of the Magento `core` modules.

You can easily add extra root items to the menu, but you have to make sure that the menu doesn't become too long. When the root menu becomes too long, it will cause layout issues for smaller screen resolutions.

# Adding an ACL

In the previous recipes, we created a backend controller action to which you can navigate. However, when you want to configure a custom admin role, you can't restrict the access to this page for a specific role. In this recipe, we will create an **ACL** (**Access Control List**) for our backend page and configure a role with restricted access to this page.

## Getting ready

Every admin user has a role. These roles contain access permissions, so you can restrict access to some user roles. In this recipe, we will add an extra permission to the roles so that we can configure the access for our previously created page.

## How to do it...

The following steps show you how you can restrict the access to a backend page for specific users:

1. The first thing we have to do is to check which ACLs are available. To know this, we can run the following command:

   ```
   wiz admin-resources
   ```

2. Or, we can navigate to the **Roles** page in the backend. This is located in **System | Permissions | Roles**. Click on **Add new role** and open the **Resources** tab. This will give you a list of all the available ACLs in the backend.

3. The second step is to add an extra ACL to it. To do this, we can add the following configuration in the adminhtml.xml file under the <config> tag:

   ```xml
   <acl>
     <resources>
       <all>
         <title>Allow Everything</title>
       </all>
       <admin>
         <children>
           <system>
             <children>
               <helloworld>
                 <title>Hellworld index page</title>
                 <sort_order>10</sort_order>
               </helloworld>
             </children>
           </system>
         </children>
       </admin>
     </resources>
   </acl>
   ```

4.  Clear your cache and reload the **Resources** page in the backend. When you search for Helloworld, you will see that there is a checkbox available for our previously created ACL as shown in the following screenshot:

At this point, our ACL is working. To verify this, we have to create a role with a user and log in to see that the user has access to the page:

5.  Create a new role on the **Roles** page in **System | Permissions**. Name it Test Helloworld and check the **Helloworld test** and **Manage Products** ACL.

6.  Create a backend user on the **Users** page at **System | Permissions**. Fill the form and add the user to the role that we have just created, as shown in the following screenshot:

7.  Log in as the new user, and you will see that this user has access only to the pages that we have configured in the role.

## How it works...

With the ACL system, it is possible to restrict backend pages for specific roles of users. For example, a product manager only has the rights to manage the products, categories, and promotion rules and the logistic partner only has access to the order pages.

> In the Magento Community Edition, it is not possible to restrict the access to the data of a specific store. For example, a logistic partner can only see the orders of Store 1. The restrictions are based on the controller actions.

When you don't create an ACL for a page, only the roles that have access to all resources can access the page. In most cases, this is the administrator. For other roles, it is not possible to access a page without an ACL.

# Extending the system configuration

When you want to save some configuration parameters for you module, you can use the Magento configuration table to save your configuration in it. You can find the configuration forms under **Configuration** in the **System** menu. In this recipe, we will add a configuration page in the system configuration with some configuration parameters.

## Getting ready

Prepare yourselves to extend the `Packt_Helloworld` module with some extra configuration. Also, connect to your database because we will have to look at some tables.

## How to do it...

The following steps describe the procedure to create extra configuration parameters in the **Configuration** page under **System**.

1. Create the following files in the `app/code/local/Packt/Helloworld/etc/` folder:
   - `system.xml`
   - `adminhtml.xml`

2. The second step is to create the configuration page. We will create a new tab in the left-hand side column under a new section. To create a section with the name `packt`, we have to add the following code in the `system.xml` file that we have just created:

```
<tabs>
  <packt>
    <label>Packt</label>
    <sort_order>400</sort_order>
  </packt>
</tabs>
```

3. To add a configuration page, we have to add the following code under the `global` tag of the `system.xml` file:

```
<sections>
  <helloworld translate="label" module="helloworld">
    <label>Helloworld</label>
    <tab>packt</tab>
    <sort_order>10</sort_order>
    <show_in_default>1</show_in_default>
    <show_in_website>1</show_in_website>
    <show_in_store>1</show_in_store>
    <groups>

    </groups>
  </helloworld>
</sections>
```

4. When you clear the cache and reload the page, the **PACKT** section with the **Helloworld** tab appears in the menu as shown in the following screenshot:

5. When you click on the link, you will see a 404 error. This is because we haven't created an ACL for this configuration section. To add an ACL, we have to add the following code in the `adminhtml.xml` file that we have created in the first step:

```xml
<?xml version="1.0" encoding="UTF-8"?>
<config>
  <acl>
    <resources>
      <all>
        <title>Allow Everything</title>
      </all>
      <admin>
        <children>
          <system>
            <children>
              <config>
                <children>
                  <helloworld translate="title"
                  module="helloworld">
                    <title>Helloworld section</title>
                  </helloworld>
                </children>
              </config>
            </children>
          </system>
        </children>
      </admin>
    </resources>
  </acl>
</config>
```

6.  We have to make sure that the ACL is added. To test this, you have to clear your cache and go to the **Roles** page at **System | Permissions**. On that page, click on the **Administrator** role, open the **Role Resources** tab, and change it to **Custom**. You will see your ACL entry in the list as shown in the following screenshot:

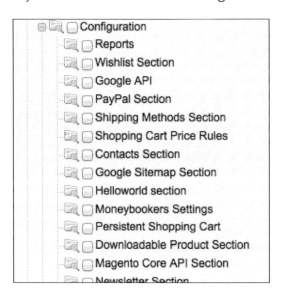

7.  When we see **Helloworld section** in the list, it means that the ACL is added. Don't save the role because this was just to verify ACL's addition. To make sure that all the ACL settings are in the backend session, we have to create a new backend session by logging out and then logging in.

 When creating an ACL, make sure that your custom ACL configuration follows the Magento XML tree where you have placed your page.

8.  When you log in again, navigate to the configuration page and you will see an empty page. It's because the fields aren't added in the configuration.

9.  A new configuration field has to be in a configuration group. To add a new group, we have to add some configuration in the `system.xml` file. Add the following code under the `config/sections/helloworld` tag:

```
<groups>
  <hellopage translate="label">
    <label>Hello page settings</label>
    <sort_order>1</sort_order>
    <show_in_default>1</show_in_default>
```

```
<show_in_website>1</show_in_website>
<show_in_store>1</show_in_store>
<fields>

</fields>
</hellopage>
</groups>
```

10. On reloading the page, you will see nothing because there are no fields defined in the `<fields>` tag. To add a field (for example, `header_title`), we have to add the following code in the `<fields>` tag:

```
<header_title translate="label">
   <label>Header title</label>
   <frontend_type>text</frontend_type>
   <sort_order>1</sort_order>
   <show_in_default>1</show_in_default>
   <show_in_website>1</show_in_website>
   <show_in_store>1</show_in_store>
</header_title>
```

11. After clearing the cache and reloading the page, you will see a field in the configuration page as shown in the following screenshot:

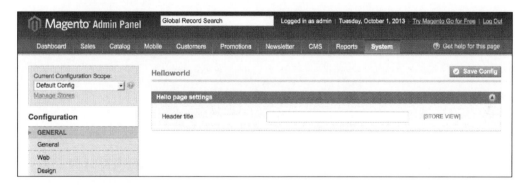

12. Enter a value in the field and save the configuration.

13. To see where the value is saved, we have to look in the `core_config_data` table. Run the following query to see the record of our field:

```
SELECT * FROM core_config_data where path = 'helloworld/hellopage/
header_title'
```

This query returns all the values of the field as shown in the following screenshot:

| config_id Config Id | scope Config Scope | scope_id Config Scope Id | path Config Path | value Config Value |
|---|---|---|---|---|
| 121 | default | 0 | helloworld/hellopage/header_title | Test value custom field |

14. To read the config data, we can use the `Mage::getStoreConfig('<path>')` function. In our case, the path is `helloworld/hellopage/header_title`. You can determine the path from the path column of the `core_config_data` table or from the `system.xml` files of the modules.

## How it works...

The Magento configuration is saved in the `core_config_data` table. This table contains all the configuration values that you can set in **System | Configuration** from the backend.

Every config setting can be configured at three levels:

▸ Global configuration

▸ Website configuration

▸ Store view configuration

When you are working with multiple stores, this setup makes it possible to save a configuration value for every store view. You can switch the scope with the drop-down field in the upper-left corner of the screen, shown as follows:

The type of every configuration value is stored in the scope column. This scope has a different code for every level:

- default (for global configuration)
- websites (for website configuration)
- stores (for stores)

For every configuration field, you can configure the scope in your `system.xml` file. This is done with the `use_in_store`, `use_in_website`, and `use_in_default` tags.

The configuration path of a configuration parameter is set in the `system.xml` files of the modules. In the following XML path, you can determine the values:

```
config/sections/$1/groups/$2/fields/$3
```

When you convert this XML path to a configuration path, it will look as follows:

```
$1/$2/$3
```

In this recipe, `$1` corresponds to `helloworld`, `$2` corresponds to `hellopage`, and `$3` corresponds to `header_title` or `is_enabled`.

# Creating a grid from a database table

In the previous chapter, we created a Magento entity that was linked to a database table. In this recipe, we will create a backend interface so that backend users can see the data from this table in the backend.

We will create an overview that will use the standard backend grid widget of Magento. This widget is widely used in the backend to display information in a grid as the **Manage Products** page.

## Getting ready

For this recipe, we have to configure a backend controller, a menu item, an ACL, and the right `Block` files to render the grid output. Prepare yourselves to extend the backend with a custom grid.

## How to do it...

1. The first thing we have to do is to create a backend controller for our grid. We will create a grid based on the subscription entity, so we will create `SubscriptionController`. Create a `SubscriptionController.php` file in the `app/code/local/Packt/Helloworld/controllers/Adminhtml/Helloworld/` folder.

2. Add the following content in the controller:

```php
<?php
class Packt_Helloworld_Adminhtml_Helloworld_SubscriptionController
extends Mage_Adminhtml_Controller_Action
{
  public function indexAction()
  {
    $this->loadLayout();

    $this->renderLayout();
  }
}
```

3. Create a menu item for the controller. When you add the following code in the `adminhtml.xml` file of the module, it will create a menu item under the **Customer** item:

```xml
<menu>
  <customer>
    <children>
      <subscription translate="title" module="helloworld">
        <title>Helloworld subscriptions</title>
        <sort_order>10</sort_order>
        <action>adminhtml/helloworld_subscription</action>
      </subscription>
    </children>
  </customer>
</menu>
```

4. Create an ACL for the controller action. This can be done by adding the following code in the same `adminhtml.xml` file as we did for the menu.

```xml
<acl>
  <resources>
    <all>
      <title>Allow Everything</title>
    </all>
    <admin>
      <children>
        <customer>
          <children>
            <subscription>
              <title>Hellworld subscriptions</title>
              <sort_order>10</sort_order>
            </subscription>
```

```
            </children>
          </customer>
        </children>
      </admin>
    </resources>
  </acl>
```

5.  Clear the cache and reload your backend. The menu item is now in the menu under **Customer**. When you navigate to the page, you will see an empty backend page.

    We now have a backend page that is linked to the menu. In the next steps, we will add a grid in the page. To do this, we have to create two blocks. The first block is for the wrapper (title, classes). The second one is for the grid where we will define the columns.

6.  To create the wrapper block, create the `app/code/local/Packt/Helloworld/Block/Adminhtml` folder. In that folder, create a `Subscription.php` file with the following content:

```php
<?php
class Packt_Helloworld_Block_Adminhtml_Subscription extends Mage_
Adminhtml_Block_Widget_Grid_Container
{
  public function __construct()
  {
    $this->_headerText = Mage::helper('helloworld')->__
    ('Helloworld subscriptions');

    $this->_blockGroup = 'helloworld';
    $this->_controller = 'adminhtml_subscription';

    parent::__construct();
  }

  protected function _prepareLayout()
  {
    $this->_removeButton('add');

    return parent::_prepareLayout();
  }
}
```

7.  Create the `app/code/local/Packt/Helloworld/Block/Adminhtml/Subscription` folder with a `Grid.php` file in it. In that file, add the following content:

```php
<?php
class Packt_Helloworld_Block_Adminhtml_Subscription_Grid extends
Mage_Adminhtml_Block_Widget_Grid
```

```
{
  public function __construct()
  {
    parent::__construct();

    $this->setId('subscription_grid');
    $this->setDefaultSort('subscription_id');
    $this->setDefaultDir('DESC');
  }

  protected function _prepareCollection()
  {
    $collection = Mage::getModel('helloworld/subscription')-
    >getCollection();
    $this->setCollection($collection);
    return parent::_prepareCollection();
  }

  protected function _prepareColumns()
  {
    $this->addColumn('subscription_id', array (
      'index' => 'subscription_id',
      'header' => Mage::helper('helloworld')->__
      ('Subscription id'),
      'type' => 'number',
      'sortable' => true,
      'width' => '100px',
    ));

    $this->addColumn('firstname', array (
      'index' => 'firstname',
      'header' => Mage::helper('helloworld')->__('Firstname'),
      'sortable' => false,
    ));

    $this->addColumn('lastname', array (
      'index' => 'lastname',
      'header' => Mage::helper('helloworld')->__('Lastname'),
      'sortable' => false,
    ));

    $this->addColumn('email', array (
      'index' => 'email',
```

```
        'header' => Mage::helper('helloworld')->__('Email'),
        'sortable' => false,
    ));

    return parent::_prepareColumns();
}

public function getGridUrl()
{
    return $this->getUrl('*/*/grid', array(
        '_current' => true,
    ));
}
}
```

8. To add the blocks to the page, add the following code in the `indexAction()` function of the previously created controller file:

```
public function indexAction()
{
    $this->loadLayout();

    $this->_addContent($this->getLayout()->createBlock('helloworld/
    adminhtml_subscription'));

    $this->renderLayout();
}
```

9. Reload the page and you will get the following output:

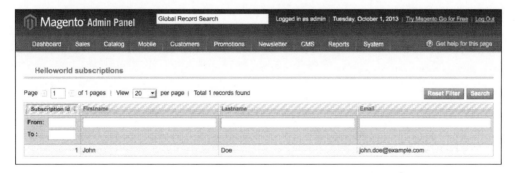

10. To change the page title, we have to go to the wrapper block class. This is the `app/code/local/Packt/Helloworld/Block/Adminhtml/Subscription.php` file. The `$this->_headerText` variable in the `__contsruct()` action contains the title of the page.

11. Now, the grid contains the **Subscription id**, **Firstname**, **Lastname**, and **Email**. In
    `_prepareColumns()`, we will add more columns to the grid so that it shows all the
    columns of the database table.

12. The `created_at` field is of the type `datetime`. When we add the following code in
    the `_prepareColumns()` function, we will see the `created_at` column with a date
    filter:

```
$this->addColumn('created_at', array (
    'index' => 'created_at',
    'header' => Mage::helper('helloworld')->  ('Created At'),
    'type' => 'datetime',
    'sortable' => true,
    'width' => '150px',
));
```

13. The last column that we will add is the **status** column. In this column, we will add
    some HTML markup to the values. For this, we need to add the following code in the
    `_prepareColumns()` function:

```
$this->addColumn('status', array (
    'index' => 'status',
    'header' => Mage::helper('helloworld')->__('Status'),
    'sortable' => true,
    'frame_callback' => array($this, 'prepareStatusLayout'),
    'width' => '150px',
));
```

14. The `frame_callback` column requires the `prepareStatusLayout()` function.
    Create the following function in the `grid` class:

```
public function prepareStatusLayout($value)
{
    $class = '';
    switch ($value) {
        case 'pending' :
            $class = 'grid-severity-notice';
            break;
        case 'approved' :
            $class = 'grid-severity-major';
            break;
        case 'declined' :
            $class = 'grid-severity-critical';
            break;
    }
    return '<span class="'.$class.'"><span>'.$value.'</span>
    </span>';
}
```

## How it works...

The backend grid is one of the backend widgets that is available in Magento. Other widgets that are widely used are the forms or the tabbed left menu. The grid widget is made to display the content of a collection in a grid, where you can sort and filter on the columns. A pager is automatically included, which prevents out-of-memory exceptions when there is a very large number of records in a collection.

The rendering of the grid is done in the `Mage_Adminhtml_Block_Widget_Grid` class. Our grid directly extends this class and overwrites the functions that were needed to customize the output for our entity.

In the `_prepareCollection()` function, we initialize the collection where we will work. The `_prepareColumns()` function is used to define the columns of the grid. In the `_prepareColumns()` function, we can play with the definition of the columns. A column definition is done with the `$this->addColumn()` function. In this function, we will initialize an array with the parameters for the column. It is recommended to use the following parameters for every column:

- `header` (column title)
- `index` (column in database)
- `sortable` (enables sorting for the column when true)

The following parameters are optional:

- `width` (defines a width for the column)
- `frame_callback` (calls a function to render the value of a cell)
- `type` (defines the filter widget such as number, datetime, and options)
- `options` (defines a source model when the type is `options`)

# Adding customer attributes

Sometimes, it is easy if we can add an attribute to a customer as we can do with products. This is possible, but there is no interface for adding attributes in the backend. We have to create it using a module that adds the attributes to the `customer` object. In this recipe, we will add a `loyaltynumber` field to the customer.

## Getting ready

For adding a `customer` attribute, the only task is to create an upgrade script which adds the attribute. Then, we have to link the attribute in the `form` table.

## How to do it...

Perform the following steps to add the `loyaltynumber` attribute to your customer objects:

1. The first step is to create the upgrade script. In the previous chapters, we have created an `install` and `upgrade` script in the `app/code/local/Packt/Helloworld/sql/helloworld_setup` folder. Create an extra install script with the name `upgrade-002-003.php`.

2. To install the `customer` attribute, add the following code in that `install` script:

```php
<?php

$installer = $this;

$installer->startSetup();

//Create the attribute "loyaltynumber" for the customer entity
$installer->addAttribute('customer', 'loyaltynumber', array(
    'type' => 'varchar',
    'input' => 'text',
    'required' => false,
    'label' => 'Loyaltynumber',
    'visible' => true,
    'adminhtml_only' => true,
    'user_defined' => true,
));

//Add the attribute to the backend forms
//@todo

$installer->endSetup();
```

This will add a `text` attribute to the `customer` entity.

3. The previous code was to create the attribute for the customer. In this step, we will add the attribute to the customer form in the backend. We can do this by adding the following code under the `@todo` comment:

```php
$loyaltyAttribute = Mage::getSingleton('eav/config')-
>getAttribute('customer', 'loyaltynumber');

$loyaltyAttribute->setData('used_in_forms', array('adminhtml_
customer'));

$loyaltyAttribute->save();
```

4. To execute the upgrade script, update the version number from `0.0.2` to `0.0.3` in `config.xml`.

5. To run the script, clear the caches and reload the page. When you navigate to a customer in the backend, you will see that the attribute is added in the form as shown in the following screenshot:

## How it works...

The installation of the `customer` attribute works in the same way as adding a `product` attribute via code. The only big difference is the entity type. Adding the field to the backend form of a customer is not as easy as for a product. For a customer, the fields to be displayed in the form are stored in the `eav_form_attribute` table.

While rendering the form, Magento will get the data from this table and render the fields based on the configuration in the attribute. The customer address is another EAV entity related to the customer entity. Adding attributes to a customer address works in the same way as adding a customer entity.

# Working with source models

Magento works with a lot of drop-down fields that you can select in the forms of the application. Also, we can make use of drop-down fields in our custom fields.

A drop-down or multiselect field always has options that you can choose in this field. To render these options, Magento uses a class that returns the options. Such a class is called a **source model**.

In this recipe, we will see which source models Magento uses and how we can create a custom source model for a custom configuration field.

## Getting ready

For this recipe, we will create a source model that is linked to a custom configuration field. This is done in the `Packt_Helloworld` module, which we will extend in this recipe.

## How to do it...

The following steps describe how you can create your own source models for your form fields.

1. The first thing that we have to create is a configuration field of the type drop-down. This has the same syntax as a normal configuration. In the `system.xml` file of the `Packt_Helloworld` module, add the following configuration under the `<fields>` tag:

```
<is_enabled translate="label">
  <label>Enabled</label>
  <frontend_type>select</frontend_type>
  <sort_order>10</sort_order>
  <show_in_default>1</show_in_default>
  <show_in_website>1</show_in_website>
  <show_in_store>1</show_in_store>
</is_enabled>
```

2. Clear your cache and go to the configuration page. You will see that there is an additional drop-down field without options. To create the options, we have to link a source model to it. The next code adds a **Yes/No** option to the field. Add this under the `is_enabled` tag:

```
<source_model>adminhtml/system_config_source_yesno</source_model>
```

3. To create our own source model, we have to create a `Model` instance. Create the `Packt_Helloworld_Model_Source_Config_Relation` class. We can do this by creating a `Relation.php` file in the `app/code/local/Packt/Helloworld/Model/Source/Config` folder. Add the following content to that file:

```
<?php
class Packt_Helloworld_Model_Source_Config_Relation
{
  public function toOptionArray()
  {
```

```
        return array(
          array(
            'value' => null,
            'label'=>Mage::helper('helloworld')->__('--Please
            Select--'),
          ),
          array(
            'value' => 'bronze',
            'label'=>Mage::helper('helloworld')->__('Bronze'),
          ),
          array(
            'value' => 'silver',
            'label'=>Mage::helper('helloworld')->__('Silver'),
          ),
          array(
            'value' => 'gold',
            'label'=>Mage::helper('helloworld')->__('Gold'),
          ),
        );
    }
}
```

4.  To link the previously created source model to the block, we have to change the
    source_model line in the system.xml file. Change the line to the following:

    `<source_model>helloworld/source_config_relation</source_model>`

5.  Clear your cache and you will see that the options of the field are changed based on
    the output from the source model, as shown in the following screenshot:

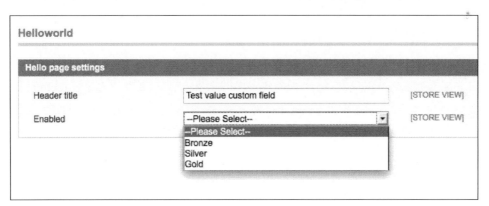

## How it works...

A source model is a model instance with a `toOptionArray()` function. This function returns an array with all the items of the source array. This array has the following format:

```
array(
  array(
    'value' => '0',
    'label' => 'Label option 0',
  ),
  array(
    'value' => '1',
    'label' => 'Label option 1',
  )
)
```

The `value` key is the value of the `<option>` in the drop-down list. The `label` key is the text that appears in the drop-down list.

In this recipe, we configured a source model for a configuration field. We can also use source models in the following cases:

- The product attribute in the backend
- The customer attribute in the backend
- The additional backend form
- The drop-down filter in backend grids

The configuration of the source model is mostly done in the configuration of the field. For EAV forms, the information of the source model is stored in the attribute configuration that is in the database.

When a drop-down or multiselect field is saved, it is always saved in a single field of the database. If a field is a drop-down, a value will be stored in that field. When the field is a multiselect field, a comma-separated list of the selected values will be saved in that field.

# 8
# Event Handlers and Cronjobs

In this chapter, we will cover the following topics:

- ▶ Understanding Magento event types
- ▶ Creating your own event
- ▶ Adding an event listener
- ▶ Introducing cronjobs
- ▶ Creating a new cronjob
- ▶ Testing your new cronjob

## Introduction

In the e-commerce flow of Magento, there are a lot of events that happen when a visitor buys something from your shop. He or she adds a product to the shopping cart, selects a payment method, logs in, and so on.

Magento dispatches these events and you have the possibility to hook in to an event to do your stuff. It's like hooking in to a click event in JavaScript.

The Observer design pattern is used to implement the event handling system. An event happens in the installation, and the configuration will call the right function from an observer class to execute.

The cronjob system in Magento is built on the same design pattern. Cronjobs are configured in the configuration. When the cron runs, Magento will check the timeframes and execute the jobs that match the configuration.

# Understanding Magento event types

Working with event listeners is better than rewriting a core class. When analyzing a process, it is good to think about how you can do it and if it is possible to work with the Magento events.

Before we can do that, we have to see which events are available, when they are dispatched, and which parameters are sent with the event.

## Getting ready

In this recipe, we will explore how the Magento event system works. We will use the Magento log system to debug a core class to see which events are available and when they are dispatched.

## How to do it...

Follow the ensuing instructions to see the event system in action:

1. When debugging something, it is recommended that you enable Magento logging. You can do this by configuring it in the backend. Navigate to **System | Configuration | Advanced | Developer**. Configure the **Enabled** parameter as shown in the following screenshot:

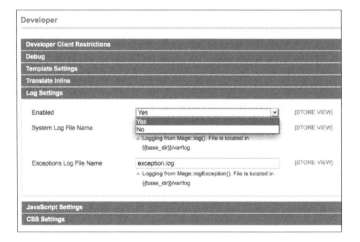

 You can also run the wiz command `wiz devel-logging yes` in your command-line tool to enable logging.

2. Magento events are dispatched with the `Mage::dispatchEvent()` function. To debug this function, we have to edit it. The `Mage::dispatchEvent()` function will call the `dispatchEvent()` function in the `app/code/core/Mage/Core/Model/App.php` file. To edit this file, we have to copy the file into the `app/code/local/Mage/Core/Model` folder. If this folder doesn't exist, create it and copy the file.

3. In that file, search for the `dispatchEvent()` function. In the first line of that function, add `Mage::log($eventName);` to print the event name in the logfile. The beginning of that function will look like the following code snippet:

```
public function dispatchEvent($eventName, $args)
{
    Mage::log($eventName);
    foreach ($this->_events as $area=>$events) {
        if (!isset($events[$eventName])) {
            $eventConfig = $this->getConfig()-
            >getEventConfig($area, $eventName);
            if (!$eventConfig) {
                $this->_events[$area][$eventName] = false;
                continue;
            }
            $observers = array();
            foreach ($eventConfig->observers->children() as
            $obsName=>$obsConfig) {
                . . .
```

4. Clear the cache and reload the page in the frontend.

5. Have a look at the `var/log/system.log` file. By using the `tail -f` command, you can see the changes of the file live. In the command line, go to the directory of your Magento installation and run the following command:

**`tail -f var/log/system.log`**

This will give you the following output:

```
~/packt/magento-dev$ tail -f var/log/system.log
+00:00 DEBUG (7): resource_get_tablename
+00:00 DEBUG (7): resource_get_tablename
+00:00 DEBUG (7): resource_get_tablename
+00:00 DEBUG (7): model_save_after
+00:00 DEBUG (7): core_abstract_save_after
+00:00 DEBUG (7): model_save_commit_after
+00:00 DEBUG (7): core_abstract_save_commit_after
+00:00 DEBUG (7): controller_front_send_response_before
+00:00 DEBUG (7): http_response_send_before
+00:00 DEBUG (7): controller_front_send_response_after
```

6. When reloading a new page, you will see that a lot of events are printed in the logfile of Magento.

7. Enough debugging for now. It is time to remove the file `app/code/local/Mage/Core/Model/App.php`.

## How it works...

The first thing we did was enable the Magento log. This is recommended for development environments because all the debug messages are printed in the file `var/log/system.log`.

>  PHP warnings and notices are also printed in this file, so it is recommended to have a look at it when developing.

To print a debug message, we used the `Mage::log()` function. The first parameter of this function is the message you want to debug. If the parameter is an object or array, Magento will print a dump of the variable in the logfile.

The second parameter is the log level. When this is not specified, the error level `DEBUG` is used. This parameter requires a numeric value. These values are set in the `const` variables of the `Zend_Log` class, which are the following:

- ▶ `Zend_Log::EMERG`
- ▶ `Zend_Log::ALERT`
- ▶ `Zend_Log::CRIT`
- ▶ `Zend_Log::ERR`
- ▶ `Zend_Log::WARN`
- ▶ `Zend_Log::NOTICE`
- ▶ `Zend_Log::INFO`
- ▶ `Zend_Log::DEBUG`

With the third parameter, you can configure a file in the `var/log` folder where the log message needs to be printed. When this parameter is empty, the default file `system.log` is used.

The fourth and last parameter is a Boolean value where you can force to always print a log message (even if the Magento logging is set to off).

When using the `Mage::log()` function, you will print the debug data without changing the output of the PHP process.

For every request in Magento, many events are dispatched. So, there are many ways to integrate and execute custom code in the Magento process.

Working with events is better than rewriting a core class of Magento. When you rewrite a core class, it is possible that your code will become incompatible while upgrading Magento or installing third-party modules.

When you work with events, you will create an extension on Magento instead of creating a modification when you rewrite a core class.

So, it is good to think about the way you want to execute custom code in Magento.

## See also

A full list of the Magento events can be found at: `http://www.magentocommerce.com/wiki/5_-_modules_and_development/reference/magento_events`.

Make sure that this list is not complete when you are working with custom modules because they can have their own events.

# Creating your own event

When we want to create our own event, we have to dispatch it with a custom name. In this recipe, we will learn how events are dispatched and what we can do with parameters that we will forward.

## Getting ready

We will create our own event that is fired when a visitor opens the `helloAction()` function of the `Packt_Helloworld` module. In this recipe, we will build further on the `Packt_Helloworld` module that is created in *Chapter 4, Creating a Module, Chapter 6, Databases and Modules*, and *Chapter 7, Magento Backend*. If you want, you can install the start files.

## How to do it...

The following steps describe how we can dispatch our own event.

1. Open the `IndexController` of the `Packt_Helloworld` module. In this controller, there is a `helloAction()` function where we will work to dispatch the event.

2. To dispatch an event, the `Mage::dispatchEvent()` function is used. When we change the code of the `helloAction()` function to the following code, we will dispatch an event called `helloworld_register_visit`:

```
public function helloAction()
{
  $this->loadLayout();
  Mage::dispatchEvent('helloworld_register_visit');

  $this->renderLayout();
}
```

3. Every time the page is reloaded, the event is dispatched. Because there is no listener added, nothing will happen. To test that the code works, you have to debug the `Mage_Core_Model_App::dispatchEvent()` function like we did in the previous recipe. You can find this function in the file `app/code/core/Mage/Core/Model/App.php`.

4. The second thing we will do is add two parameters to the event. For example, we will send a product and a category to the event. We will use the second parameter to send the parameters. This parameter accepts a key value array with the objects. The following code shows how to send parameters to the event:

```
public function helloAction()
{
    $this->loadLayout();
    $parameters = array(
        'product' => Mage::getModel('catalog/product')-
        >load(166),
        'category' => Mage::getModel('catalog/category')-
        >load(10),
    );
    Mage::dispatchEvent('helloworld_register_visit',
    $parameters);
    $this->renderLayout();
}
```

 Make sure the product and category ID exists in your webshop. If not, you can use another ID that exists in your webshop.

## How it works...

The `Mage::dispatchEvent()` function fires an event in Magento. When this function is called, Magento will look into the configuration and execute the matching event observer functions, also known as observers in the Magento world.

You can use the `Mage::dispatchEvent()` function in every context you want, so it's to you to decide where you want to place it if needed.

# Adding an event observer

An event listener (observer) is used when you want to hook in to an event. In the previous recipe, we fired an event. In this recipe, we will catch events and look at how we can execute custom code when the event occurs in the website.

## Getting ready

For this recipe, we will add two event observers. The first one will catch the event that we created in the previous recipe. The second event listener (observer) will hook into the "add to cart" action of a product.

## How to do it...

The following steps describe what you can do with event observers:

1. To listen to the `helloworld_register_edit` event, we have to add configuration to the `config.xml` file of the `Packt_Helloworld` module. Add the following code in this file under the `<global>` tag:

```
<events>
   <helloworld_register_visit>
      <observers>
         <register_visit>
            <type>singleton</type>
            <class>helloworld/observer</class>
            <method>registerVisit</method>
         </register_visit>
      </observers>
   </helloworld_register_visit>
</events>
```

2. We just configured an observer that fires the `registerVisit()` function of the `helloworld/observer` class. We have to create the `Packt_Helloworld_Model_Observer` class. Create the file `app/code/local/Packt/Helloworld/Model/Observer.php` with the following content:

```
<?php
class Packt_Helloworld_Model_Observer
{
    public function registerVisit (Varien_Event_Observer
    $observer)
    {
       Mage::log('Registered');
    }
}
```

3. We can test the event observer by firing the event. The event is fired on the page `http://magento-dev.local/helloworld/index/hello`. Navigate to this file and check the debug messages in the Magento logfile (`var/log/system.log`).

4. The observer function prints a debug message in the Magento logfile. Let's look at the parameters that we send with the event. These parameters are sent in the `$observer` object in the function. To get the product and the category, change the `registerVisit()` action to the following code to debug the product and category:

```
public function registerVisit ($observer)
{
   $product = $observer->getProduct();
   $category = $observer->getCategory();
```

```
        Mage::log($product->debug());
        Mage::log($category->debug());
    }
```

5. For the next part, we will hook in to the "add to cart" event. When a user adds a product to the cart, we have to check that the quantity is odd. If not, we have to show an error message that the product can't be added to the cart.

6. To do that, we have to create an event listener (observer) for the event `checkout_cart_product_add_after`. We do this by adding the following code in the `config.xml` file of the `Packt_Helloworld` module. Paste the following code under the `<events>` tag:

```
<checkout_cart_product_add_after>
  <observers>
    <check_cart_qty>
      <type>singleton</type>
      <class>helloworld/observer</class>
      <method>checkCartQty</method>
    </check_cart_qty>
  </observers>
</checkout_cart_product_add_after>
```

7. This will call the `checkCartQty()` function in the observer class. The following code will display a notice message when the event is fired:

```
public function checkCartQty ($observer)
{
    Mage::getSingleton('checkout/session')-
    >addNotice('Product add event fired');
}
```

8. Clear your cache and add a product to the cart. The message will appear in the cart page when a product is added, as shown in the following screenshot:

9.  Now, we have to add the following code to check if the quantity is odd or even. This code gets the quantity from the observer and adds a check for even or odd:

```
public function checkCartQty ($observer)
{
    if ($observer->getProduct()->getQty() % 2 == 0) {
        //Even
    } else {
        //Odd
    }
}
```

10. When the quantity is even, we have to show a notice. When the quantity is odd, we have to cancel the "add to cart" operation and display a message. We can do this by throwing an exception. In an event observer, we can never use return values. To work correctly, the check function will look like the following code:

```
public function checkCartQty (Varien_Event_Object $observer)
{
    if ($observer->getProduct()->getQty() % 2 == 0) {
        //Even
        Mage::getSingleton('checkout/session')->addNotice('Even
        quantity added');
    } else {
        //Odd
        Mage::throwException('Quantity is odd. It needs to be
        even');
    }
}
```

11. Clear the cache and add a product to the cart with an even and odd quantity. You will see that the odd quantity will result in an error message.

## How it works...

Event listeners (observers) are always configured in the `config.xml` file. When we look at the configuration, every tag has its own purpose:

```
<events>
  <helloworld_register_visit>
    <observers>
      <register_visit>
        <type>singleton</type>
        <class>helloworld/observer</class>
        <method>registerVisit</method>
      </register_visit>
```

```
        </observers>
      </helloworld_register_visit>
    </events>
```

The `<events>` tag is the root to define events in it. The `<events>` tag can be configured under the `<global>`, `<frontend>`, or `<admin>` tags depending on the scope of the event that needs to be executed.

Under the `<events>` tag, we find the `<helloworld_register_visit>` tag. The name of the tag is the name of the event that will be observed. The observers are defined in the child tags.

Under the `<helloworld_register_visit>` tag, you see an `<observers>` subtag. In this tag, all the observers are declared.

In this recipe, we have a `register_visit` observer. The observers that are declared under the `<observers>` tag needs to have a unique name. When using an existing name, you will overwrite the configuration of an `existing` observer.

The observer tag (`register_visit`) has the following subtags:

> ▸ `<type>`: This is the design pattern to call the class, mostly as `singleton` or `model`
> ▸ `<class>`: This is the Magento path to the class
> ▸ `<method>`: This is the method to be executed

The previous event will execute the configured class and function when the event is fired with the `dispatchEvent()` function.

To every observer function, an `$observer` object is passed. This variable is an instance of the `Varien_Event_Observer` class. This class extends the `Varien_Object` class and it contains some extra event-related functions.

The return parameters of the event observer functions will be ignored. When working with an event observer, you have to look at the context where the `Mage::dispatchEvent()` function is placed.

Sometimes, it is placed in a `try-catch` structure like the `checkout_cart_product_add_after` event in this recipe. In other cases, you can change the values of the passed objects like the `model_save_before` event does.

# Introducing cronjobs

Cronjobs or scheduled tasks are background processes that keep your Magento webshop running. Some examples of cronjobs are as follows:

> ▸ Sending newsletters
> ▸ Recalculating catalog promotion rules for the next day

- ▸ Cleaning visitor logs
- ▸ Sending product stock and price alert mails
- ▸ Updating currency rates

If cronjobs are not configured on the server, you will see issues with your webshop after a period of time.

## Getting ready

In this recipe, we will learn how to configure cronjobs on the server and verify that they are working. Make an SSH connection to your server and prepare yourselves to perform some server configurations.

## How to do it...

The following steps describe how you have to configure the cronjobs on your server:

1. Practically, we have to configure cronjobs every five minutes. For that to happen, the following command is executed:

   ```
   /bin/sh /var/www/packt/magento-dev/cron.sh
   ```

 To avoid permission problems, you have to run this command as the user that apache uses to serve the HTTP requests. In our setup, this user is `www-data`.

2. When you execute the previous command, the cronjob table in the database is updated with the recent cronjobs. In the `cron_schedule` table, you can see the queue for the next 30 minutes. Run the following command in your database client to see the content of the table:

   ```
   SELECT * from CRON_SCHEDULE;
   ```

   This query gives you the following output:

| schedule_id Schedule Id | job_code Job Code | status Status | messages Messages | created_at Created At | scheduled_at Scheduled At | executed_at Executed At | finished_at Finished At |
|---|---|---|---|---|---|---|---|
| 11 | captcha_delete_old_attempts | pending | NULL | 2013-10-09 19:14:17 | 2013-10-09 19:30:00 | NULL | NULL |
| 12 | captcha_delete_expired_images | pending | NULL | 2013-10-09 19:14:17 | 2013-10-09 19:20:00 | NULL | NULL |
| 13 | captcha_delete_expired_images | pending | NULL | 2013-10-09 19:14:17 | 2013-10-09 19:30:00 | NULL | NULL |
| 14 | newsletter_send_all | pending | NULL | 2013-10-09 19:14:17 | 2013-10-09 19:15:00 | NULL | NULL |
| 15 | newsletter_send_all | pending | NULL | 2013-10-09 19:14:17 | 2013-10-09 19:20:00 | NULL | NULL |
| 16 | newsletter_send_all | pending | NULL | 2013-10-09 19:14:17 | 2013-10-09 19:25:00 | NULL | NULL |
| 17 | newsletter_send_all | pending | NULL | 2013-10-09 19:14:17 | 2013-10-09 19:30:00 | NULL | NULL |
| 18 | xmlconnect_notification_send_all | pending | NULL | 2013-10-09 19:14:17 | 2013-10-09 19:15:00 | NULL | NULL |
| 19 | xmlconnect_notification_send_all | pending | NULL | 2013-10-09 19:14:18 | 2013-10-09 19:20:00 | NULL | NULL |
| 20 | xmlconnect_notification_send_all | pending | NULL | 2013-10-09 19:14:18 | 2013-10-09 19:25:00 | NULL | NULL |
| 21 | xmlconnect_notification_send_all | pending | NULL | 2013-10-09 19:14:18 | 2013-10-09 19:30:00 | NULL | NULL |

3. In the `scheduled_at` column, you see when the cronjob is planned to run. When running the `cron.sh` script after the `scheduled_at` time, we have to run the query again. This will give the following output:

| schedule_id Schedule Id | job_code Job Code | status Status | messages Messages | created_at Created At | scheduled_at Scheduled At | executed_at Executed At | finished_at Finished At |
|---|---|---|---|---|---|---|---|
| 11 | captcha_delete_old_attempts | pending | NULL | 2013-10-09 19:14:17 | 2013-10-09 19:30:00 | NULL | NULL |
| 12 | captcha_delete_expired_images | pending | NULL | 2013-10-09 19:14:17 | 2013-10-09 19:20:00 | NULL | NULL |
| 13 | captcha_delete_expired_images | pending | NULL | 2013-10-09 19:14:17 | 2013-10-09 19:30:00 | NULL | NULL |
| 14 | newsletter_send_all | success | NULL | 2013-10-09 19:14:17 | 2013-10-09 19:15:00 | 2013-10-09 19:18:48 | 2013-10-09 19:18:48 |
| 15 | newsletter_send_all | pending | NULL | 2013-10-09 19:14:17 | 2013-10-09 19:20:00 | NULL | NULL |
| 16 | newsletter_send_all | pending | NULL | 2013-10-09 19:14:17 | 2013-10-09 19:25:00 | NULL | NULL |
| 17 | newsletter_send_all | pending | NULL | 2013-10-09 19:14:17 | 2013-10-09 19:30:00 | NULL | NULL |
| 18 | xmlconnect_notification_send_all | success | NULL | 2013-10-09 19:14:17 | 2013-10-09 19:15:00 | 2013-10-09 19:18:48 | 2013-10-09 19:18:48 |
| 19 | xmlconnect_notification_send_all | pending | NULL | 2013-10-09 19:14:18 | 2013-10-09 19:20:00 | NULL | NULL |
| 20 | xmlconnect_notification_send_all | pending | NULL | 2013-10-09 19:14:18 | 2013-10-09 19:25:00 | NULL | NULL |
| 21 | xmlconnect_notification_send_all | pending | NULL | 2013-10-09 19:14:18 | 2013-10-09 19:30:00 | NULL | NULL |

4. To run a cronjob, we have to use the crontab file on the Linux server. To configure it, we have to switch to the `www-data` user. We can do this by running the following command:

```
sudo su www-data
```

5. Next, we have to configure the cronjob. We can do this by running the `crontab -e` command. This will open a file where we have to put the content shown in the following screenshot:

```
# Edit this file to introduce tasks to be run by cron.
#
# Each task to run has to be defined through a single line
# indicating with different fields when the task will be run
# and what command to run for the task
#
# To define the time you can provide concrete values for
# minute (m), hour (h), day of month (dom), month (mon),
# and day of week (dow) or use '*' in these fields (for 'any').#
# Notice that tasks will be started based on the cron's system
# daemon's notion of time and timezones.
#
# Output of the crontab jobs (including errors) is sent through
# email to the user the crontab file belongs to (unless redirected).
#
# For example, you can run a backup of all your user accounts
# at 5 a.m every week with:
# 0 5 * * 1 tar -zcf /var/backups/home.tgz /home/
#
# For more information see the manual pages of crontab(5) and cron(8)
#
# m h  dom mon dow   command
*/5 * * * * /bin/sh /var/www/packt/magento-dev/cron.sh
```

6.  Save the file and the cronjob will run every five minutes.

## How it works...

The Magento cron script is called the `cron.sh` file in the Magento root folder. This will execute the `cron.php` file over **Command Line Interface (CLI)**. In this `cron.php` file, the Magento application is started and the cron process is initialized.

When the cron process is initialized, Magento will look at the `cron_schedule` table. Every scheduled cronjob with the `scheduled_at` field in the past will be executed. When a job starts, the `executed_at` field will be updated to the current timestamp.

When a job is finished, the `finished_at` field is updated with the current timestamp. Also, the status will be updated. When the status is an error, the message field will be updated with the error.

When the process is finished, Magento will create a queue for the next 30 minutes. Based on the configuration files, Magento knows which cronjob has to be scheduled each time.

# Creating a new cronjob

The cronjobs are defined in the `config.xml` files of the Magento modules. Like every configuration in these files, the cronjob configuration is easy to extend in our own module. In this recipe, we will learn how to create extra cronjobs for the Magento installation.

## Getting ready

The workflow to execute a cronjob is mostly the same as working with events. We have to configure an observer function in the `config.xml` file that will be executed when the cronjob is executed.

In the `Packt_Helloworld` module, we will create a cronjob that will save some data in the database.

## How to do it...

Follow the ensuing steps to see which configuration is needed to configure an extra cronjob:

1.  We have to create a crontab configuration in the `config.xml` file. The following configuration will do that. Paste this under the `<config>` tag of the file `app/code/local/Packt/Helloworld/etc/config.xml`:

```
<crontab>
  <jobs>
    <helloworld_check_subscriptions>
```

```
            <schedule>
              <cron_expr>* 10 * * *</cron_expr>
            </schedule>
            <run>
              <model>helloworld/observer::checkSubscriptions
              </model>
            </run>
          </helloworld_check_subscriptions>
        </jobs>
      </crontab>
```

2.  Clear the cache and verify that the configuration is working by running the following command in your terminal:

    `wiz config-get crontab/jobs`

    This command gives you a list of all the configured cronjobs in the configuration.

    If the `helloworld_check_subscriptions` code is under the list, it means that the configuration is working.

3.  When the configuration is OK, we have to create the observer function. In the run/model tag, we will call the `cronListener()` action in the class `Packt_Helloworld_Model_Observer`. Create the class if it is not there and add the `checkSubscriptions()` function in it. The function will look like the following code:

```
public function checkSubscriptions()
{
  $subscription = Mage::getModel('helloworld/subscription');
  $subscription->setFirstname('Cron');
  $subscription->setLastname('Job');
  $subscription->setEmail('cron.job@example.com');
  $subscription->setMessage('Created by cronjob');

  $subscription->save();
}
```

    This will save a `subscription` entity in the `subscriptions` table when the cron is executed.

## How it works...

When you look at the cronjob configuration, the first XML tag you see is the cronjob code. This has to be unique across all the modules. If it exists, you will overwrite the settings of an existing standard cronjob.

A good practice is to start the cronjob code with the name that you used to register the models of your module (`helloworld`, `catalog`, and so on). This code is followed with the action you want to do.

> A cronjob code is always in small letters. Spaces are replaced by an underscore.

One level deeper, you see the `<schedule>` and `<run>` tags.

In the `<schedule>` tag, we can configure the interval of the cronjob. This configuration contains five parameters which represent the following configurations:

- Minute
- Hour
- Day
- Month
- Year

A configuration such as `0 10 * * *` will run every day at 10:00 a.m. This means every weekday, every month, every day, at hour 10 and minute 0.

The `<run>` tag just initializes the observer class and function to call when a cron needs to be executed. It is not possible to send parameters to that function.

# Testing your new cronjob

When you are developing a new cronjob, it is not so easy to test it. You will not wait until the cron will be executed because you will lose a lot of time to do it.

On **Magento Connect**, there is a module that makes the testing of a cronjob easy. This module allows you to run a cronjob from the backend or command line.

It also adds a view to the backend that is a graphical representation of the `cron_schedule` table.

## Getting ready

We will install a module from Magento Connect on our Magento installation. More information of the module can be found at: `http://www.magentocommerce.com/magento-connect/aoe-scheduler.html`.

## How to do it...

The following steps describe the workflow of the module to test cronjobs:

1. Install the module by getting the extension key from Magento Connect. Be sure to take the key for **Magento Connect 2.0** as shown in the following screenshot:

2. Paste the extension key in Magento Connect Manager. Navigate to **System | Magento Connect | Magento Connect Manager**, paste the extension key, and click on the **Install** button as shown in the following screenshot:

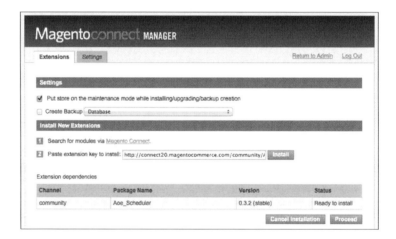

3. When you proceed, Magento Connect Manager will install the module to the installation.

It is possible that Magento Connect Manager fails to install the module. If it does, you can use the website `http://freegento.com/ddl-magento-extension.php` to download a ready-to-paste format of the module.

4. When you return to the admin, you will see that there is a menu item added under the **System** section. When you navigate to **System | Scheduler | Schedule Configuration**, you will see a list of all available cronjobs.

5. To run a cronjob, you have to select one in the grid. After that, select **Run now** in the drop-down above the grid and click on **Submit**. This will directly run your cronjob.

6.  When you navigate to **System | Scheduler | Timeline View**, you will see the information about the cronjob in the timeline as shown in the following screenshot:

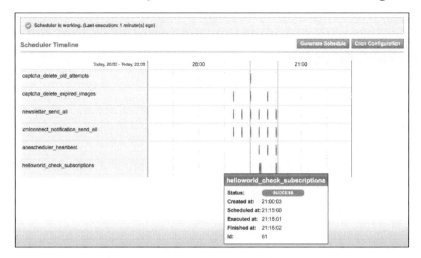

7.  In the `shell` folder of the Magento root, the module adds a shell script to test the cronjobs by command line. This is the `scheduler.php` file, which has the following options:

    ❑  action (`runNow` or `scheduleNow`)

    ❑  code (the cronjob code)

8.  To run our cronjob by command line, the command looks like the following when you are in the Magento root folder:

    **php shell/scheduler.php -action runNow -code cronjob_code**

9.  The previous command directly runs the cronjob. When you want to schedule the cronjob with the current timestamp (so it will be executed when the next cron runs), we have to use the `scheduleNow` action. With this option, the command looks like the following:

    **php shell/scheduler.php -action scheduleNow -code cronjob_code**

## How it works...

The `Aoe_Scheduler` module adds an interface to the backend to simplify the process to test a cronjob. It is just a graphical interface on the `cron_schedule` table.

When you are working with cronjobs in your module, this module is recommended and saves a lot of time.

The shell script is added to test the cronjobs over the command line. Make sure when you run a cronjob over PHP CLI or you run it in the browser, other PHP settings are used. An Apache request uses the Apache php.ini settings and the command-line PHP uses the PHP CLI settings.

# 9
# Creating a Shipping Module

In this chapter, we will cover the following topics:

- ▶ Initializing module configurations
- ▶ Writing an adapter model
- ▶ Extending the shipping method features
- ▶ Adding the module in the frontend

## Introduction

Shipping ordered products to customers is one of the key parts of the e-commerce flow. In most cases, a shop owner has a contract with a shipping handler where everyone has their own business rules.

In a standard Magento, the following shipping handlers are supported:

- ▶ DHL
- ▶ FedEx
- ▶ UPS
- ▶ USPS

If your handler is not on the list, have a look if there is a module available at Magento Connect. If not, you can configure a standard shipping method or you can create your own, which we will do in this chapter.

# Initializing module configurations

In *Chapter 4, Creating a Module*, we learned how we can create a custom module. In this recipe, we will create the necessary files for a shipping module, which we will extend with more features using the recipes of this chapter.

## Getting ready

Open your code editor with the Magento project. Also, get access to the backend where we will check some things.

## How to do it...

The following steps describe how we can create the configuration for a shipping module:

1. Create the following folders:

   - `app/code/local/Packt/`
   - `app/code/local/Packt/Shipme/`
   - `app/code/local/Packt/Shipme/etc/`
   - `app/code/local/Packt/Shipme/Model/`
   - `app/code/local/Packt/Shipme/Model/Carrier`

2. Create the module file named `Packt_Shipme.xml` in the folder `app/etc/modules` with the following content:

   ```xml
   <?xml version="1.0"?>
   <config>
     <modules>
       <Packt_Shipme>
         <active>true</active>
         <codePool>local</codePool>
         <depends>
           <Mage_Shipping />
         </depends>
       </Packt_Shipme>
     </modules>
   </config>
   ```

3. Create a `config.xml` file in the folder `app/code/local/Packt/Shipme/etc/` with the following content:

   ```xml
   <?xml version="1.0" encoding="UTF-8"?>
   <config>
   ```

```
<modules>
  <Packt_Shipme>
    <version>0.0.1</version>
  </Packt_Shipme>
</modules>

<global>
  <models>
    <shipme>
      <class>Packt_Shipme_Model</class>
    </shipme>
  </models>
</global>

<default>
  <carriers>
    <shipme>
      <active>1</active>
      <model>shipme/carrier_shipme</model>
      <title>Shipme shipping</title>

      <express_enabled>1</express_enabled>
      <express_title>Express delivery</express_title>
      <express_price>4</express_price>

      <business_enabled>1</business_enabled>
      <business_title>Business delivery</business_title>
      <business_price>5</business_price>
    </shipme>
  </carriers>
</default>

</config>
```

4. Clear the cache and navigate in the backend to **System | Configuration | Advanced | Disable Modules Output**. Observe that the `Packt_Shipme` module is on the list.

5. At this point, the module is initialized and working. Now, we have to create a `system.xml` file where we will put the configuration parameters for our shipping module. Create the file `app/code/local/Packt/Shipme/etc/system.xml`.

6.  In this file, we will create the configuration parameters for our shipping module. When you paste the following code in the file, you will create an extra group in the shipping method's configuration. In this group, we can set the settings for the new shipping method:

```xml
<?xml version="1.0" encoding="UTF-8"?>
<config>
  <sections>
    <carriers>
      <groups>
        <shipme translate="label" module="shipping">
          <label>Shipme</label>
          <sort_order>15</sort_order>
          <show_in_default>1</show_in_default>
          <show_in_website>1</show_in_website>
          <show_in_store>1</show_in_store>
          <fields>
            <!-- Define configuration fields below -->

            <active translate="label">
              <label>Enabled</label>
              <frontend_type>select</frontend_type>
              <source_model>adminhtml/
              system_config_source_yesno</source_model>
              <sort_order>10</sort_order>
              <show_in_default>1</show_in_default>
              <show_in_website>1</show_in_website>
              <show_in_store>1</show_in_store>
            </active>

            <title translate="label">
              <label>Title</label>
              <frontend_type>text</frontend_type>
              <sort_order>20</sort_order>
              <show_in_default>1</show_in_default>
              <show_in_website>1</show_in_website>
              <show_in_store>1</show_in_store>
            </title>

          </fields>
        </shipme>
      </groups>
    </carriers>
  </sections>
</config>
```

7. Clear the cache and navigate in the backend to the shipping method configuration page. To do that, navigate to **System | Configuration | Sales | Shipping methods**. You will see that an extra group is added as shown in the following screenshot:

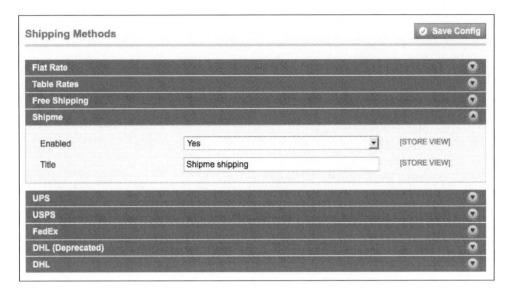

8. You will see that there is a new shipping method called **Shipme**. We will extend this configuration with some values. Add the following code under the `<fields>` tag of the module:

```
<active translate="label">
    <label>Enabled</label>
    <frontend_type>select</frontend_type>
    <source_model>adminhtml/system_config_source_yesno
    </source_model>
    <sort_order>10</sort_order>
    <show_in_default>1</show_in_default>
    <show_in_website>1</show_in_website>
    <show_in_store>1</show_in_store>
</active>

<title translate="label">
    <label>Title</label>
    <frontend_type>text</frontend_type>
    <sort_order>20</sort_order>
    <show_in_default>1</show_in_default>
    <show_in_website>1</show_in_website>
    <show_in_store>1</show_in_store>
</title>
```

```xml
<express_enabled translate="label">
  <label>Enable express</label>
  <frontend_type>select</frontend_type>
  <source_model>adminhtml/system_config_source_yesno
  </source_model>
  <sort_order>30</sort_order>
  <show_in_default>1</show_in_default>
  <show_in_website>1</show_in_website>
  <show_in_store>1</show_in_store>
</express_enabled>

<express_title translate="label">
  <label>Title express</label>
  <frontend_type>text</frontend_type>
  <sort_order>40</sort_order>
  <show_in_default>1</show_in_default>
  <show_in_website>1</show_in_website>
  <show_in_store>1</show_in_store>
</express_title>

<express_price translate="label">
  <label>Price express</label>
  <frontend_type>text</frontend_type>
  <sort_order>50</sort_order>
  <show_in_default>1</show_in_default>
  <show_in_website>1</show_in_website>
  <show_in_store>1</show_in_store>
</express_price>

<business_enabled translate="label">
  <label>Enable business</label>
  <frontend_type>select</frontend_type>
  <source_model>adminhtml/system_config_source_yesno
  </source_model>
  <sort_order>60</sort_order>
  <show_in_default>1</show_in_default>
  <show_in_website>1</show_in_website>
  <show_in_store>1</show_in_store>
</business_enabled>

<business_title translate="label">
  <label>Title business</label>
  <frontend_type>text</frontend_type>
```

```
            <sort_order>70</sort_order>
            <show_in_default>1</show_in_default>
            <show_in_website>1</show_in_website>
            <show_in_store>1</show_in_store>
        </business_title>

        <business_price translate="label">
            <label>Price business</label>
            <frontend_type>text</frontend_type>
            <sort_order>80</sort_order>
            <show_in_default>1</show_in_default>
            <show_in_website>1</show_in_website>
            <show_in_store>1</show_in_store>
        </business_price>
```

9. Clear the cache and reload the backend. You will now see the other configurations under the **Shipme – Express** shipping method as shown in the following screenshot:

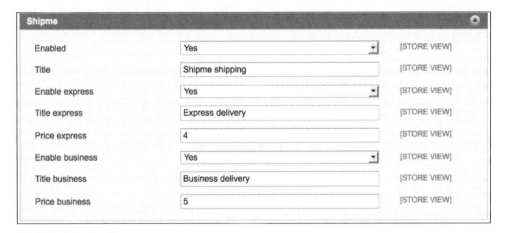

## How it works...

The first thing we have done is to create the necessary files to initialize the module. The following files are required to initialize a module:

- ▸ `app/etc/modules/Packt_Shipme.xml`
- ▸ `app/code/local/Packt/Shipme/etc/config.xml`

In the first file, we will activate the module with the `<active>` tag. The `<codePool>` tag describes that the module is located in the local code pool, which represents the folder `app/code/local/`.

In this file, there is also the `<depends>` tag. First this will check if the `Mage_Shipping` module is installed or not. If not, Magento will throw an exception. If the module is available, the dependency will load this module after the `Mage_Shipping` module. This makes it possible to rewrite some values from the `Mage_Shipping` module.

In the second file, `config.xml`, we configured all the stuff that we will need in this module. These are the following things:

- The version number (`0.0.1`)
- The models
- Some default values for the configuration values

The last thing we did was create a `system.xml` file so that we can create a custom configuration for the shipping module.

The configuration in the `system.xml` file adds some extra values to the shipping method configuration, which is available in the backend under the menu **System | Configuration | Sales | Shipping methods**.

In this module, we created a new shipping handler called `Shipme`. Within this handler, you can configure two shipping options: **express** and **business**. In the `system.xml` file, we created the fields to configure the visibility, name, and price of the options.

## See also

In this recipe, we used the `system.xml` file of the module to create the configuration values. You can find information about this in the *Extending the system configuration* recipe from *Chapter 7, Magento Backend*.

# Writing an adapter model

A new shipping module is initialized in the previous recipe. What we did in the previous recipe was a preparation to continue with the business part we will see in this recipe. We will add a model with the business logic for the shipping method. The model is called an **adapter** class because Magento requires an adapter class for each shipping method. This class will extend the `Mage_Shipping_Model_Carrier_Abstract` class.

This class will be used for the following things:

- Make the shipping method available
- Calculate the shipping costs
- Set the title in the frontend of the shipping methods

## How to do it...

Perform the following steps to create the adapter class for the shipping method:

1. Create the folder `app/code/local/Packt/Shipme/Model/Carrier` if it doesn't already exist.

2. In this folder, create a file named `Shipme.php` and add the following content to it:

```php
<?php
class Packt_Shipme_Model_Carrier_Shipme
    extends Mage_Shipping_Model_Carrier_Abstract
    implements Mage_Shipping_Model_Carrier_Interface
{
    protected $_code = 'shipme';

    public function collectRates
    (Mage_Shipping_Model_Rate_Request $request)
    {
        $result = Mage::getModel('shipping/rate_result');

        //Check if express method is enabled
        if ($this->getConfigData('express_enabled'))
        {
            $method = Mage::getModel
            ('shipping/rate_result_method');
            $method->setCarrier($this->_code);
            $method->setCarrierTitle
            ($this->getConfigData('title'));

            $method->setMethod('express');
            $method->setMethodTitle
            ($this->getConfigData('express_title'));

            $method->setCost
            ($this->getConfigData('express_price'));
            $method->setPrice
            ($this->getConfigData('express_price'));

            $result->append($method);
        }

        //Check if business method is enabled
        if ($this->getConfigData('business_enabled'))
```

```
    {
        $method = Mage::getModel
        ('shipping/rate_result_method');
        $method->setCarrier($this->_code);
        $method->setCarrierTitle
        ($this->getConfigData('title'));

        $method->setMethod('business');
        $method->setMethodTitle
        ($this->getConfigData('business_title'));

        $method->setCost
        ($this->getConfigData('business_price'));
        $method->setPrice
        ($this->getConfigData('business_price'));

        $result->append($method);
    }

    return $result;
}

public function isActive()
{
    $active = $this->getConfigData('active');
    return $active==1 || $active=='true';
}

public function getAllowedMethods()
{
    return array('shipme'=>$this->getConfigData('name'));
}
}
```

3. Save the file and clear the cache; your adapter model has now created.

## How it works...

The previously created class handles all the business logic that is needed for the shipping method. Because this adapter class is an extension of the `Mage_Shipping_Model_Carrier_Abstract` class, we can overwrite some methods to customize the business logic of the standard.

The first method we overwrite is the `isAvailable()` function. In this function, we have to return `true` or `false` to say that the module is active. In our code, we will activate the module based on the system configuration field `active`.

The second method is the `collectRates()` function. This function is used to set the right parameters for every shipping method. For every shipping method, we can set the title and price.

The class implements the interface `Mage_Shipping_Model_Carrier_Interface`. In this interface, two functions are declared: the `isTrackingAvailable()` and `getAllowedMethods()` functions.

We created the function `getAllowedMethods()` in the adapter class. The `isTrackingAvailable()` function is declared in the parent class `Mage_Shipping_Model_Carrier_Abstract`.

We configured two options under the **Shipme** shipping method. These options are called **Express delivery** and **Business delivery**. We will check if they are enabled in the configuration and set the configured title and price for each option.

The last thing to do is return the right values. We have to return an instance of the class `Mage_Shipping_Model_Rate_Result`. We created an empty instance of the class, where we will append the methods to when they are available.

To add a method, we have to use the function `append($method)`. This function requires an instance of the class `Mage_Shipping_Model_Rate_Result_Method` that we created in the two `if` statements.

# Extending the shipping method features

When all the files are installed, we can add more features to the shipping method. In this recipe, we will add a country configuration and we will enable tracking codes for the shipping method.

## How to do it...

Perform the following steps to tracking codes and country-specific shipping:

1. Open the adapter file `app/code/local/Packt/Shipme/Model/Carrier/Shipme.php`.

2. Add the following function in this file to enable tracking codes:

```
public function isTrackingAvailable()
{
    return true;
}
```

Tracking codes are now enabled for the `Shipme` shipping methods.

3. To enable country-specific shipping, we have to add some configuration fields in the `system.xml` file of the module. Add the following code as the child of the `<fields>` tag:

```
<sallowspecific translate="label">
  <label>Ship to Applicable Countries</label>
  <frontend_type>select</frontend_type>
  <sort_order>90</sort_order>
  <frontend_class>shipping-applicable-country</frontend_class>
  <source_model>adminhtml/system_config_source_shipping
_allspecificcountries</source_model>
  <show_in_default>1</show_in_default>
  <show_in_website>1</show_in_website>
  <show_in_store>0</show_in_store>
</sallowspecific>

<specificcountry translate="label">
  <label>Ship to Specific Countries</label>
  <frontend_type>multiselect</frontend_type>
  <sort_order>100</sort_order>
  <source_model>adminhtml/system_config_source_country
</source_model>
  <show_in_default>1</show_in_default>
  <show_in_website>1</show_in_website>
  <show_in_store>0</show_in_store>
  <can_be_empty>1</can_be_empty>
</specificcountry>
```

4. Clear the cache and open the configuration page of the shipping method. You will see that there are two new configuration options. When you change **Ship to Applicable Countries** to **Specific Countries**, you can select multiple countries as seen in the following screenshot:

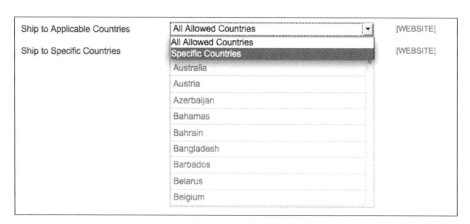

## How it works...

The first thing we did was enable the possibility to create tracking codes for the `Shipme` shipping method. We overwrote the `isTrackingAvailable()` function, which returns the standard `false`. By returning `true`, we enable the tracking codes.

The second thing we did was enable country-specific shipping. We configured two fields with a standard naming convention. When we enable the configuration in the backend, we can only use the shipping method when the shipping address is in one of the selected countries.

# Adding the module in the frontend

In this recipe, we will test that the shipping method appears in the frontend. We prepared the code and configuration in the previous recipes to make this possible.

## How to do it...

In this recipe, we will check the configuration and place a test order with the new shipping method:

1. Log in to the admin panel.
2. Navigate to the shipping methods page by going to **System | Configuration | Sales | Shipping methods**.
3. Check that all the values are correct for the **Shipme – Express** method. Also make sure it is enabled.
4. Save the configuration.
5. Go to the frontend, add a product to the shopping cart, and checkout.
6. Fill in the right data for the billing and shipping steps.

7. In the shipping method step, new methods will appear as shown in the following screenshot:

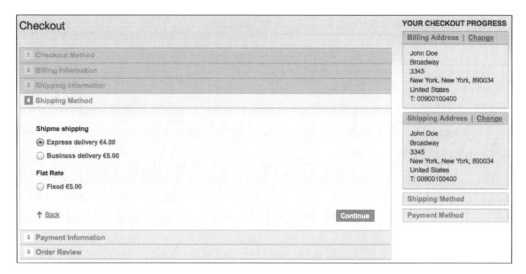

8. Select a method from the list and click on the **Continue** button.

9. In the payment method step, choose the **Check Money Order** method.

 If you don't see the **Check Money Order** payment method, you have to enable it in the system configuration.

10. Click **Continue** and place the order. You will see the success page.

11. In the backend, go to **Sales | Orders** and click on the latest order.

12. To complete the order, we have to create an invoice for it to confirm that the order is paid. When you click on the **Invoice** button, you will be redirected to the invoice form where you can submit your invoice.

13. When the invoice is saved, you will see that the status of the order has changed to **Processing**. When the status is **Processing**, you can click on the **Ship** button to create the shipment. You will see the following screen:

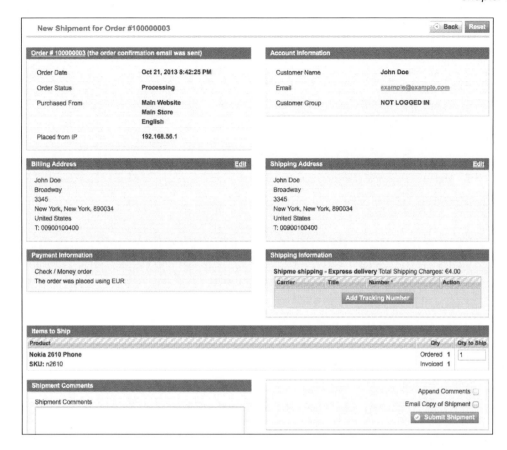

14. When you click on the **Add Tracking Number** button, choose the **Shipme shipping** option from the drop-down and add a tracking code such as 1234567890:

15. When you click on the **Submit Shipment** button, your shipment is processed and the status of the order will change to **Complete**.

## How it works...

In this recipe, we tested the shipping method that we created in this chapter. We placed an order with the new shipping method to check that everything works the way we wanted it to.

# 10
# Creating a Product Slider Widget

In this chapter, we will cover the following topics:

- ▶ Creating an empty module
- ▶ Registering helpers and blocks
- ▶ Creating a widget configuration file
- ▶ Creating a block and the template files
- ▶ Creating a custom configuration parameter
- ▶ Finalizing the theming

## Introduction

Magento widgets are graphical interfaces to configure blocks in the frontend. For every widget, there is a configuration page available where you can set the required values for that widget.

When the configuration is done, you can configure the layout instructions to show the widget at several places in the frontend.

In this recipe, we will create a new module where we will create our own widget. We will create a product slider with the products of a category that we can configure in the widget.

When we have performed the required configuration for the widget, we will finish the representation in the frontend. We will create a product list that we will style with a jQuery slider script.

# Creating an empty module

As we did in the previous chapter and fully explained in *Chapter 4, Creating a Module*, we will create the required files to create an empty module that we will extend with widget configurations in further chapters.

We will start with an empty Magento module that we will create in this recipe. We will create all the required files to initialize a new module that can be used for the creation of a widget.

## Getting ready

Open your code editor and prepare yourselves to create a new module called `Packt_Productslider`.

## How to do it...

When you perform the following steps, you will create an empty `Packt_Productslider` module:

1. Create the following folders for the module:
   - `app/code/local/`
   - `app/code/local/Packt/`
   - `app/code/local/Packt/Productslider/`
   - `app/code/local/Packt/Productslider/etc`

2. Create the module file `Packt_Productslider.xml` in the `modules` folder under `app/etc`.

3. Paste the following code into it:

```xml
<?xml version="1.0"?>
<config>
  <modules>
    <Packt_Productslider>
      <active>true</active>
      <codePool>local</codePool>
      <depends>
        <Mage_Widget />
      </depends>
    </Packt_Productslider>
  </modules>
</config>
```

4. Create the configuration file for the module. This is the `config.xml` file that is located in the `etc` folder under `app/code/local/Packt/Productslider`.

5. Add the following content to the file:

```xml
<?xml version="1.0" encoding="UTF-8"?>
<config>
  <modules>
    <Packt_Productslider>
      <version>0.0.1</version>
    </Packt_Productslider>
  </modules>
</config>
```

6. Clear the cache and check whether the module is installed. You can do this by navigating to the configuration page, **System** | **Configuration** | **Advanced** | **Advanced**, and checking whether the module is on the list. Alternatively, you can run the command `wiz module-list` in the command line.

## How it works...

We just created a new module with the name `Packt_Productslider`. This module is a custom module, so we configured it in the local code pool.

Practically, this module does nothing, but we will extend it in the next recipes.

# Registering helpers and blocks

The widget module we will create uses a custom block. For translating strings in the block and in different configurations, we need to configure a helper class.

## Getting ready

We will initialize blocks and helpers, and we will create the default helper for our module, just like we did in *Chapter 4, Creating a Module*.

## How to do it...

The following steps describe how to configure helpers and blocks for a new module.

1. Create the following folders:
   - `app/code/local/Packt/Productslider/Block`
   - `app/code/local/Packt/Productslider/Helper`

2.  In the `config.xml` file of the module, add the following configuration under the `<config>` tag:

```xml
<global>
  <blocks>
    <productslider>
      <class>Packt_Productslider_Block</class>
    </productslider>
  </blocks>
  <helpers>
    <productslider>
      <class>Packt_Productslider_Helper</class>
    </productslider>
  </helpers>
</global>
```

3.  Create the `Data.php` file under `app/code/local/Packt/Productslider/Helper` and paste the following content into it:

```php
<?php
class Packt_Productslider_Helper_Data extends Mage_Core_Helper_
Abstract
{

}
```

4.  Clear the cache, and your blocks and helpers will be registered.

## How it works...

In the previous code, we initialized blocks and helpers with the name `productslider`. With this configuration, it is possible to use block names such as `productslider/block_name`.

The helpers are also registered under the name `productslider`. We created a default helper, which we can call with the function `Mage::helper('productslider')`.

# Creating a widget configuration file

In this recipe, we will configure a new widget type. We have to create a new configuration file where we will initialize the following things for the widget type:

▶  Name of the widget (in the backend)

▶  Widget configuration parameters

▶  Widget block type

▶  Widget templates (`.phtml` files)

## Getting ready

To test the widget configuration, we can navigate to the **Widgets** page under **CMS** in the backend to manage the widget instances.

## How to do it...

Perform the following steps to create a `widget.xml` configuration file.

1. Create the file `app/code/local/Packt/Productslider/etc/widget.xml`.

2. Add the following code to this file:

```xml
<?xml version="1.0" encoding="UTF-8"?>
<widgets>
  <category_product_slider type="catalog/product_list">
    <name>Category product slider</name>
    <description>Displays the products for a given category
    in a slider widget</description>
  </category_product_slider>
</widgets>
```

3. Clear your cache and check whether the configuration works.

4. At the backend, navigate to **CMS | Widgets**, click on the **Add New Widget Instance** button, and confirm that the widget is in the list, as shown in the following screenshot:

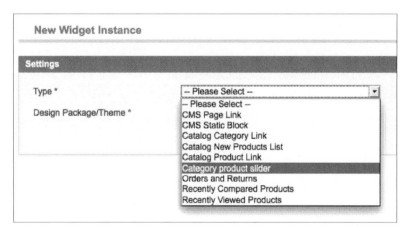

5. Configure the widget for your frontend theme and go to the next page.

6. You are now on the widget configuration page. In the **Widget Options** tab, we will create our own widget parameters.

7. To create a title field that we will use in the block, we have to create a `parameters` tag as shown in the following code. Paste this under the `<category_product_slider>` tag.

```
<parameters>
    <title>
        <label>Title (frontend)</label>
        <type>text</type>
        <required>1</required>
        <visible>1</visible>
    </title>
</parameters>
```

8. Clear the cache, reload the backend page, and go to the **Widget Options** tab. You will see that there is a title field available, as shown in the following screenshot:

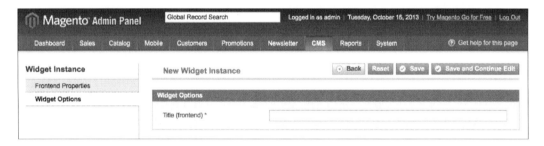

9. To show all the products of a category, we have to create a configuration where we can select a category. We will create a text field where we can paste the right category ID. To configure the field, add the following code under the `<parameters>` tag:

```
<category_id>
    <label>Category ID</label>
    <type>text</type>
    <required>1</required>
    <sort_order>20</sort_order>
    <visible>1</visible>
</category_id>
```

10. Clear the cache and reload the page again. You will see that a second textbox is added to the configuration form.

## How it works...

The `widget.xml` file is used to define widgets in the Magento installation. All widget types in Magento are defined under the `<widgets>` configuration tag.

Under this tag, we defined a new widget called `category_product_slider`. In this tag, we used the `type` attribute to define the `Block` class that the widget will refer to. In this case, it is `catalog/product_list`. This is the block that is used to render the category product list or the grid.

Under the `<category_product_slider>` tag, we have used the following configuration tags:

- name
- description
- parameters

The `name` tag is used for the widget type name that is used in the dropdown when creating a widget.

The `description` tag is for information. It is not shown in the frontend or backend. It is only used for providing information for the widget.

In the `parameters` tag, we define the configuration parameters for the widget. In our case, these are `name` and `category_id`.

Our fields are just text fields, but we can also make use of other input fields such as dropdowns and checkboxes. When working with dropdown or multiselect fields, we can define a source model with the `<source_model>` tag.

# Creating a block and the template files

In the previous chapters, we learned how we can configure the widget. Now it is time to show the widget.

We will create a custom block where we will write a query that returns the products for the given category, and we will set up a configuration to use two template files on the widget configuration page.

## Getting ready

We will work further to create our own widget instance. Open the `widget.xml` file that we created in the previous recipe.

## How to do it...

The following steps describe how we configure a custom block with custom templates for the widget instance.

1. First, we will create a block class that extends the `Mage_Catalog_Block_Product_List` class. We do this because the behavior of that class is what we need for our widget.

2. Create the `List.php` file under `app/code/local/Packt/Productslider/Block/Catalog/Product`.

3. Add the following content to that file to initialize the class and the functions that we will configure:

```php
<?php
class Packt_Productslider_Block_Catalog_Product_List
extends Mage_Catalog_Block_Product_List
implements Mage_Widget_Block_Interface
{
  protected function _beforeToHtml()
  {
    parent::_beforeToHtml();
  }

  protected function _prepareLayout()
  {
    parent::_prepareLayout();
  }
}
```

4. Configure the block that uses the class we previously created. We do this by changing the `type` attribute in the `<category_product_slider>` tag. Change the attribute to `productslider/catalog_product_list`.

5. When the block class is created, it is time to create templates for the block. In this widget, we will use two templates. The first template comprises the image, title, and price of the products. The second template only shows the image and the **Add To Cart** button.

6. Create the templates in the `category-product-slider` folder under `app/design/frontend/base/default/template/productslider`.

7. Create the folder and add the following files to this folder:

   ❑ `list.phtml`
   ❑ `teaser.phtml`

8. In the `list.phtml` file, add the following content:

```
<div class="block">
  <div class="block-title">
    <h2><?php echo $this->getTitle() ?></h2>
  </div>
  <div class="block-content">
    <p>Test of the list.phtml template</p>
  </div>
</div>
```

9. In the `teaser.phtml` file, add the following content:

```
<div class="block">
  <div class="block-title">
    <h2><?php echo $this->getTitle() ?></h2>
  </div>
  <div class="block-content">
    <p>Teasers template</p>
  </div>
</div>
```

10. Configure the widget configuration page so that you can choose your template. We can do this by adding the following as a child of the `<parameters>` tag:

```
<template>
  <label>Frontend template</label>
  <type>select</type>
  <values>
    <list translate="label">
      <value>productslider/category-product-
      slider/list.phtml</value>
      <label>List template</label>
    </list>
    <teaser translate="label">
      <value>productslider/category-product-
      slider/teaser.phtml</value>
      <label>Teaser template</label>
    </teaser>
  </values>
  <sort_order>30</sort_order>
  <visible>1</visible>
</template>
```

11. Clear the cache and go to the widget configuration page. When you click on **Add Layout Update**, you can select the page where the widget will display. The last dropdown is the template you can use for the widget, as shown in the following screenshot:

 Make sure you choose the right theme to configure the widget. We will use the default / default theme to configure the widget, so make sure your shop is using the same theme.

12. Complete the form to place a widget instance on the home page.

13. When you clear the cache, the widget will appear on the home page with the content of the chosen template file.

14. When you enable developer hints, you will see that our previously created custom block is used as shown in the following screenshot:

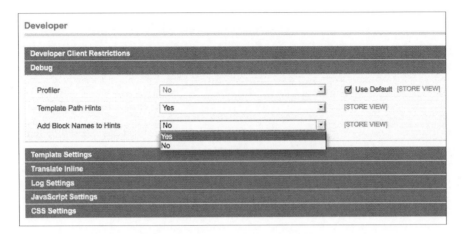

You can enable developer hints in the backend by navigating to the **Developer** page under **System | Configuration | Advanced** in the **Debug** section. Be sure to configure it on the website or store a view scope.

You can also run the wiz command `wiz devel-showhints yes` to enable the hints.

15. The last thing we will do is to create a loop that shows the name of the products. Add the following code to the `list.phtml` file:

```php
<?php $_productCollection = $this->getLoadedProductCollection() ?>
<div class="block">
  <div class="block-title">
    <h2><?php echo $this->getTitle() ?></h2>
  </div>
  <div class="block-content">
    <p><?php echo $this->__('Category ID: %s',
    $this->getCategoryId()) ?></p>
    <ul>
    <?php foreach ($_productCollection as $_product): ?>
    <li><?php echo $_product->getName() ?></li>
    <?php endforeach; ?>
    </ul>
  </div>
</div>
```

16. Configure the widget to use the right template and a valid category ID. After that, reload the frontend, and you will see something like the following screenshot:

>  You can find the category ID while navigating to a category in the backend. Navigate to **Catalog | Manage Categories**, select any category, and you will see the ID near the name.

## How it works...

We created a custom block class for the widget. By configuring the `type` attribute of the widget, all instances of this widget will use a block of the type `productslider/catalog_product_list`.

When we have a look at this class, we see that the class will extend the `Mage_Catalog_Block_Product_List` class, which is the block that is used to render product lists for a category. We use this class so we can use the standard functions instead of writing our own.

The next thing we did was to make it possible to choose two templates for the widgets. This is done by configuring the `<template>` parameter on the widget.

The template is configured in the **Layout Update** section of the widget configuration page. This form is a graphical implementation of the layout XML configuration in the template files.

When we save the widget, Magento will create a layout update in the database for the widget. This layout update is stored in the table `core_layout_update`.

When we look at the template file, we see the `$this->getTitle()` function is used to fill the title tag of the block. This function will output the data that is set for the `title` parameter on the block.

In the configuration, we created a `<title>` configuration which will do a `setData('title')` on the background when the block is created.

The second configuration parameter is the `<category_id>` field. When the category ID is set on this block, the `$this->getLoadedProductCollection()` function will return the products of the given category ID, which is just the thing we need for this case.

# Creating a custom configuration parameter

The widget is created. It shows up in the frontend and the right products are shown for the given category ID.

To configure the category ID, we have to copy it from the category page and paste it in the textbox. For better usability, we will create a custom widget in the configuration field where we can select a category from a pop-up window.

## Getting ready

To prepare yourselves, look at how you can configure the category for the **Catalog Category Link** widget in the backend. We will configure the same pop-up window for the widget that we created in previous recipes.

## How to do it...

Perform the following steps to and you can create a custom configuration parameter:

1. When we look at the **Catalog Category Link** widget, we see that they use a custom widget to select the category—we will do the same for our module.

2. In the `widget.xml` file, replace the `<category_id>` configuration parameter with the following code:

```
<category_id>
  <label>Category</label>
  <type>label</type>
  <helper_block>

<type>adminhtml/catalog_category_widget_chooser</type>
    <data>
      <button translate="open">
        <open>Select Category...</open>
      </button>
    </data>
  </helper_block>
  <required>1</required>
  <sort_order>20</sort_order>
  <visible>1</visible>
</category_id>
```

3. Clear the cache and reload the widget configuration page. You will see something like the following screenshot when you click on the configuration parameter button:

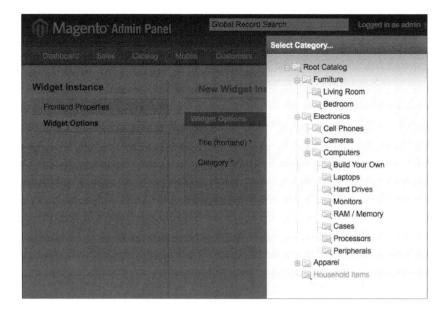

4. When you select a category, save the widget, clear the cache, and reload the home page, and you will see that the widget shows the wrong products.

5. When you inspect the **Select Category ...** button and navigate to the hidden field that is some elements above, you will see that the value is similar to `category/<category_id>`.

6. The widget requires the category ID, that is, the number after the slash. We now have the category path that is used to generate URLs. To fix this problem, we can perform the following:

   ❑ Get the ID from the path with string functions

   ❑ Make sure a proper ID is set in the widget configuration page

7. We will adapt the second method because it is the most stable way.

8. To fix the issue, we have to update some code in the category widget chooser that is shown in the widget configuration page. We will create a new class that extends the current widget chooser. We will add the class to the `Widget` folder under `app/code/local/Packt/Productslider/Block/Adminhtml/Category`.

9. In this folder, create a file called `Chooser.php` with the following content:

```php
<?php
class Packt_Productslider_Block_Adminhtml_Catalog_Category_Widget_
Chooser extends Mage_Adminhtml_Block_Catalog_Category_Widget_
Chooser
```

```
{
    /**
     * Block construction
     * Defines tree template and init tree params
     */

  public function prepareElementHtml(Varien_Data_Form_Element_
Abstract $element)
  {
    $uniqId = Mage::helper('core')->uniqHash($element-
    >getId());
    $sourceUrl = $this->getUrl('adminhtml/
    productslider_catalog_category_widget/chooser',
    array('uniq_id' => $uniqId, 'use_massaction' =>
    false));

    $chooser = $this->getLayout()-
    >createBlock('widget/adminhtml_widget_chooser')
      ->setElement($element)
      ->setTranslationHelper($this->getTranslationHelper())
      ->setConfig($this->getConfig())
      ->setFieldsetId($this->getFieldsetId())
      ->setSourceUrl($sourceUrl)
      ->setUniqId($uniqId);

    if ($element->getValue()) {
      $categoryId = $element->getValue();

      if ($categoryId) {
        $label = Mage::getSingleton('catalog/
        category')->load($categoryId)->getName();
        $chooser->setLabel($label);
      }
    }

    $element->setData('after_element_html',
    $chooser->toHtml());
    return $element;
  }

  public function getNodeClickListener()
  {
    if ($this->getData('node_click_listener')) {
      return $this->getData('node_click_listener');
```

```
    }
    if ($this->getUseMassaction()) {
      $js = '
        function (node, e) {
          if (node.ui.toggleCheck) {
            node.ui.toggleCheck(true);
          }
        }
      ';
    } else {
      $chooserJsObject = $this->getId();
      $js = '
        function (node, e) {
          '.$chooserJsObject.'.setElementValue
          (node.attributes.id);
          '.$chooserJsObject.'.setElementLabel(node.text);
          '.$chooserJsObject.'.close();
        }
      ';
    }
    return $js;
  }
}
```

10. In the previous step, we created a new block class to handle the return value of the chosen category. In this step, we will configure the configuration page to use the new block. In the `widget.xml` file of the module, change the tag `parameters/category_id/helper_block/type` from `adminhtml/catalog_category_widget_chooser` to `productslider/adminhtml_catalog_category_widget_chooser`. The `widget.xml` file will now appear as follows:

```xml
<?xml version="1.0" encoding="UTF-8"?>
<widgets>
  <category_product_slider
  type="productslider/catalog_product_list">
    <name>Category product slider</name>
    <description>Displays the products for a given category
    in a slider widget</description>
    <parameters>
      <title>
        <label>Title (frontend)</label>
        <type>text</type>
        <required>1</required>
        <sort_order>10</sort_order>
        <visible>1</visible>
```

```
        </title>
        <category_id>
          <label>Category</label>
          <type>label</type>
          <helper_block>
            <type>productslider/adminhtml_catalog_category_
            widget_chooser</type>
            <data>
              <button translate="open">
                <open>Select Category...</open>
              </button>
            </data>
          </helper_block>
          <required>1</required>
          <sort_order>20</sort_order>
          <visible>1</visible>
        </category_id>
        <template>
          <label>Frontend template</label>
          <type>select</type>
          <values>
            <list translate="label">
              <value>productslider/category-product-
              slider/list.phtml</value>
              <label>List template</label>
            </list>
            <teaser translate="label">
              <value>productslider/category-product-
slider/teaser.phtml</value>
              <label>Teaser template</label>
            </teaser>
          </values>
          <sort_order>30</sort_order>
          <visible>1</visible>
        </template>
      </parameters>
    </category_product_slider>
  </widgets>
```

11. We need a custom controller action to handle the AJAX call of the pop-up window. To initialize admin controllers for the module, add the following code to the `config.xml` file of the module. Paste it as a child of the `<config>` tag:

```
<admin>
  <routers>
    <adminhtml>
```

```
            <args>
              <modules>
                <productslider before="Mage_Adminhtml">
                Packt_Productslider_Adminhtml</productslider>
              </modules>
            </args>
          </adminhtml>
        </routers>
    </admin>
```

12. In the `Category` folder under `app/code/local/Packt/Productslider/Adminhtml/Productslider/Catalog`, create a `WidgetController.php` file with the following content in it:

```php
<?php
require_once('Mage/Adminhtml/controllers/Catalog/Category/
WidgetController.php');

class Packt_Productslider_Adminhtml_Productslider_Catalog_
Category_WidgetController extends Mage_Adminhtml_Catalog_Category_
WidgetController
{
  protected function _getCategoryTreeBlock()
  {
    return $this->getLayout()->createBlock('productslider/
    adminhtml_catalog_category_widget_chooser', '', array(
      'id' => $this->getRequest()->getParam('uniq_id'),
      'use_massaction' => $this->getRequest()
      ->getParam('use_massaction', false)
    ));
  }
}
```

13. Clear the cache and load the configuration page. Select a category in the pop-up window and inspect the hidden field as we did in step 5. You will see that the category ID is set as a number instead of a path.

14. Save the widget, clear the cache, and reload the home page. You will see that the right products of the configured category are shown.

## How it works...

In this recipe, we created a custom configuration parameter. We did this for a better user experience.

First, we configured an existing configuration widget to show a category pop-up window when clicking on the field. This was not so difficult because the only workload is to configure the right settings in the `widget.xml` file.

But this widget was not exactly what we were looking for. The frontend representation was OK, but in the background, a wrongly formatted category ID was returned.

To solve this, we created a custom configuration field that extends the previous configuration field. We only changed the required things to format the right output.

Because the widget is working with an AJAX call, we had to create a custom controller that extends the standard one to show the right block. In that controller, we included the relative path of the parent controller because this class is not in the autoloader of Magento.

## There's more...

We configured the widget parameter in this recipe to show how to create a custom HTML output for a configuration field.

Technically, you can do the most impossible things with a configuration field; however, the only thing you need to know is that you have to set the configuration value in an input field that has the naming convention: `<input name="parameter[<parameter_name>]" />`.

Replace the `<parameter_name>` tag with the name of your custom parameter and the form will handle your configuration parameter just as it handles all the others.

# Finalizing the theming

The widget we made in the frontend does not invite us to buy some products. It is just a list with the names of the products from a category.

In this recipe, we will finalize the theming of the widget. We will create an HTML output that shows an image, name, and price of the given products.

With a jQuery plugin, we will convert the HTML output to a slider so we can scroll through the products.

## Getting ready

Search for a good jQuery carousel on the Internet. In this recipe, we will use `http://caroufredsel.dev7studios.com/`.

## How to do it...

The following steps describe the last set of actions to complete the widget:

1. Let's generate a good HTML that is usable for the jQuery plugin. Add the following code to the `list.phtml` template:

```php
<?php $_productCollection = $this->getLoadedProductCollection() ?>
<div class="block-image-slider">
  <div class="block-title">
    <h2><?php echo $this->getTitle() ?></h2>
  </div>
  <div class="productslider-container">
    <div id="productslider-<?php echo $this-
    >getCategoryId() ?>">
      <?php foreach ($_productCollection as $_product): ?>
      <div class="slider-item">
        <a href="<?php echo $_product->getProductUrl() ?>"
        title="<?php echo $this->stripTags($this->
        getImageLabel($_product, 'small_image'),
        null, true)        ?>" class="carousel-image">
        <img src="<?php echo $this->helper('catalog/image')
        ->init($_product,'small_image')->resize(250); ?>"
        width="250" height="250" alt="<?php echo $this-
        >stripTags($this->getImageLabel($_product,
        'small_image'), null, true) ?>" /></a>
        <div class="slider-item-content">
          <p>
            <?php echo $_product->getName() ?>
          </p>
          <?php echo $this->getPriceHtml($_product) ?>
        </div>
        </div>
      <?php endforeach; ?>
    </div>
    <div class="productslider-controls">
      <a id="btn-prev-<?php echo $this->getCategoryId() ?>"
      class="btn-prev" href="#">&lt;</a>
      <a id="btn-next-<?php echo $this->getCategoryId() ?>"
      class="btn-next" href="#">&gt;</a>
      <div id="pager-<?php echo $this->getCategoryId() ?>"
      class="pager"></div>
    </div>
  </div>
</div>
```

2. Create a CSS file to set the required styling. Add a `productslider.css` file to the `css` folder under `skin/frontend/base/default` with the following content:

```
.productslider-container {width:700px;background-color:#DDD;}

.productslider-container .slider-item {width:250px;padding:20px;ma
rgin:20px;background-color:#BBB;float:left;clear:none;}

.productslider-container .productslider-controls
{overflow:hidden;}
.productslider-container .productslider-controls .btn-prev
{float:left;}
.productslider-container .productslider-controls .btn-next
{float:right;}
.productslider-container .productslider-controls .pager {text-
align: center;}
.productslider-container .productslider-controls .pager a
{margin:0 10px;}
```

3. Add the CSS file to the Magento head by adding the following code. With this code, the CSS file is only added when the widget is configured on a page. `app/code/local/Packt/Productslider/Block/Catalog/Product/List.php` in the `_prepareLayout()` function:

```
protected function _prepareLayout()
{
    $this->getLayout()->getBlock('head')->addCss('css/productslider.
css');

    parent::_prepareLayout();
}
```

4. Save all the files, clear the cache, and reload the frontend. You will see a styled output that we can use to convert to a slider.

5. The next step is to add a jQuery carousel script to the product list. We will use the script `http://caroufredsel.dev7studios.com/`.

6. Download the source files, unzip it, and paste the folder and content to the folder `skin/frontend/base/default/js`.

7. Link the CSS and JavaScript files by updating the `_prepareLayout()` function in the `app/code/local/Packt/Productslider/Block/Catalog/Product/List.php` file. Replace the function with the following code:

```
protected function _prepareLayout()
{
    $this->getLayout()->getBlock('head')->addCss('css/productslider.
css');
```

```
$this->getLayout()->getBlock('head')->addItem('skin_js',
'js/carouFredSel-6.2.1/jquery.carouFredSel-6.2.1-
packed.js');

    parent::_prepareLayout();
}
```

> Make sure jQuery is enabled in your theme. You can find instructions on it in *Chapter 2, Theming*.

8. The last step is to initialize the script for the product list element. Add the following JavaScript code at the bottom of the `list.phtml` template:

```
<script type="text/javascript">

jQuery(document).ready(function(){
  jQuery("#productslider-<?php echo $this->
  getCategoryId() ?>").carouFredSel({
    width: '100%',
    prev: '#btn-prev-<?php echo $this->getCategoryId() ?>',
    next: '#btn-next-<?php echo $this->getCategoryId() ?>',
    pagination: '#pager-<?php echo $this->
    getCategoryId() ?>'
  });
});

</script>
```

9. Clear the cache and reload the frontend. You're done and the output will be as shown in the following screenshot:

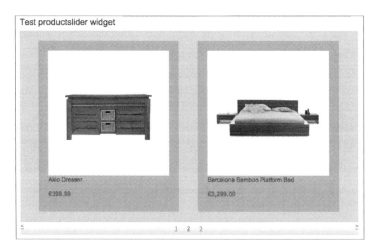

## How it works...

In the initial steps, we created a good HTML output for the template. This output generates a scaled image, title, and price for every product in the loop.

To theme the HTML output, we used a CSS file that will only be included when a widget is configured for the given page. The function `_prepareLayout()` is called when all blocks are initialized. In this function, we add a CSS file and later a JavaScript file to the head of the website.

To show the product slider with animations, we added some JavaScript code that adds the slider to the product list.

# 11
# Performance Optimization

In this chapter, we will cover the following topics:

- ▸ Exploring the limits of a website
- ▸ Optimizing the database and MySQL configuration
- ▸ Optimizing the Apache web server
- ▸ Tuning the Magento configurations
- ▸ Configuring APC and Memcached
- ▸ Optimizing the PHP configurations
- ▸ Analyzing the page speed

## Introduction

For athletes, seconds, milliseconds, or hundredths of seconds decide if they will win a competition or not. Every small aspect that improves the performance is a step in the right direction to win the competition.

For websites, it is the same. The faster your Magento store is, the better it is. Magento is not one of the most efficient systems when it comes to performance. Especially when you are working with a lot of products and attributes, a good setup improves the performance of your webshop.

The performance of a website has a lot of impact on your visitors. Some facts about this statement are listed as follows:

- The page speed has a significant influence on the page ranking in search engines such as Google
- On an e-commerce site, every second costs 1 percent of the sales total
- You get more visitors from search engines when you reduce the page size

As you can see, performance is a key part to improve the SEO of your website. Customers will leave your website when it does not show a good performance.

Since you have finished the development, it is time to take a look at the performance of the whole system. In this chapter, we will explore, detect, and fix performance leaks in a Magento webshop by using many tools.

Some tools are delivered by Magento as standard, but we have to look at the whole picture. Two identical Magento installations can have different page speed results that are caused by the following reasons:

- Hardware
- Network
- Load
- Device of the client

# Exploring the limits of a website

One of the first things you need to know are the limits of the current website. How much capacity has my website got? What is slowing down my site? We have to get an overview of all these aspects to arrive at a conclusion of which optimizations will have the most effect.

In this recipe, we will see some tools that help to create a view of the performance. Some of the tools are listed as follows:

- ApacheBench
- Siege
- Magento Profiler
- YSlow
- PageSpeed
- GTmetrix
- WebPagetest

We will do some tests with all these tools to work out the pitfalls of a Magento store. With these results, we can find out what kind of optimizations have the most effect.

Some optimizations are very easy and can have a large effect. Other optimizations are difficult and can have less effect. It is on you to decide what you want.

## Getting ready

To start, it is recommended to install the following tools to do some performance tests on a Magento installation:

- ▶ **ApacheBench** (**ab**): This tool is automatically installed with the Apache web server. When you have access to the command line interface, you can run the following command on a Linux server:

  ```
  ab -h
  ```

- ▶ **Siege**: We will do some performance tests with Siege that is installed on the same server as Magento. To see if it is installed, you can run the following command:

  ```
  siege -V
  ```

  - ❑ Here, make sure that V is uppercase. When Siege is installed, you will see its version number as shown in the following screenshot:

  ```
  SIEGE 2.70

  Copyright (C) 2010 by Jeffrey Fulmer, et al.
  This is free software; see the source for copying conditions.
  There is NO warranty; not even for MERCHANTABILITY or FITNESS
  FOR A PARTICULAR PURPOSE.
  ```

  - ❑ If it is not installed, you can run the following command when you are using a Debian-based Linux distribution:

  ```
  sudo apt-get install siege
  ```

  - ❑ A second option is to download the installation file and install it by performing the following procedure:

    1. To download the archive, run the following command:

    ```
    wget ftp://ftp.joedog.org/pub/siege/siege-latest.tar.gz
    ```

    2. To extract the archive, run the following command:

    ```
    tar xzf siege-latest.tar.gz
    ```

    3. Move the folder to the preferred location and change the directory.

4.  Install Siege with the following command:

```
sudo ./configure
```

- ▸ **Magento Profile**: This is a standard feature in Magento. You can enable it in your system's configuration.

- ▸ **YSlow**: This is a Firefox plugin that you can download and install from the Add-ons store.

Because **GTMetrix** and **WebPagetest** are online tools, we don't have to install them.

## How to do it...

1.  To get an idea of the response time under a load of concurrent users, we can use ApacheBench. We will perform a test with the following command and save the results to a CSV file:

```
ab -c 10 -n 50 -e apachebench.csv http://magento-dev.local/
```

2.  In the previous command, we did a load test with the following parameters:

- ❑  -c: This parameter represents the number of concurrent users. In this test, there were always 10 requests running at the same time.

- ❑  -n: This parameter represents the number of requests. In this case it is 50, so we will have 50 results in the file.

- ❑  -e: This parameter represents the output file. The output is written to the given CSV file.

 The -g option means the same as -e but -g will generate a .tsv (**tab separated value**) file, also known as a gnuplot file.

3.  When you run the command, an output screen with the results will be printed as shown in the following screenshot:

```
Benchmarking magento-dev.local (be patient).....done


Server Software:        Apache/2.2.20
Server Hostname:        magento-dev.local
Server Port:            80

Document Path:          /
Document Length:        27346 bytes

Concurrency Level:      1
Time taken for tests:   21.302 seconds
Complete requests:      50
Failed requests:        0
Write errors:           0
Total transferred:      1391100 bytes
HTML transferred:       1367300 bytes
Requests per second:    2.35 [#/sec] (mean)
Time per request:       426.031 [ms] (mean)
Time per request:       426.031 [ms] (mean, across all concurrent requests)
Transfer rate:          63.77 [Kbytes/sec] received

Connection Times (ms)
              min  mean[+/-sd] median   max
Connect:        0    0   0.1      0       1
Processing:   307  425 535.7    341    4130
Waiting:      285  403 532.6    319    4086
Total:        307  426 535.8    341    4131

Percentage of the requests served within a certain time (ms)
  50%    341
  66%    345
  75%    351
  80%    368
  90%    394
  95%    465
  98%   4131
  99%   4131
 100%   4131 (longest request)
```

This report shows the general statistics of the test. The specific results are saved in the CSV file.

4. When you run the `ab -h` command, you will see all the available options.

5. Load testing with Siege.

   Siege is another load testing tool like ApacheBench. The difference between Siege and ApacheBench is that Siege has more functions than ApacheBench. It is designed to do a stress test with a number of concurrent users. It has the ability to work with HTTP authentication, cookies, sessions, and more. When you write a good script, you can simulate a real stress situation.

6. For a load test with Siege, we will use a text file, where we will set some URLs that will be used during the Siege load test. Doing a test with different URLs is better because you will test more pages on your website, which means that you can find more pitfalls. Create a `siege_url.txt` file and paste the following content in it:

- `http://magento-dev.local/`
- `http://magento-dev.local/skin/frontend/default/default/images/bkg_body.gif`
- `http://magento-dev.local/skin/frontend/default/default/images/logo.gif`
- `http://magento-dev.local/skin/frontend/default/default/images/ph_callout_left_top.gif`
- `http://magento-dev.local/skin/frontend/default/default/images/ph_callout_left_rebel.jpg`
- `http://magento-dev.local/skin/frontend/default/default/images/home_main_callout.jpg`
- `http://magento-dev.local/index.php/electronics.html`
- `http://magento-dev.local/index.php/electronics.html?cat=12`
- `http://magento-dev.local/index.php/checkout/cart/add/product/46/`
- `http://magento-dev.local/index.php/checkout/cart/`
- `http://magento-dev.local/skin/frontend/default/default/images/i_shipping.gif`
- `http://magento-dev.local/skin/frontend/default/default/images/i_discount.gif`
- `http://magento-dev.local/skin/frontend/default/default/images/btn_trash.gif`
- `http://magento-dev.local/skin/frontend/default/default/images/bkg_th.gif`
- `http://magento-dev.local/skin/frontend/default/default/images/i_msg-success.gif`
- `http://magento-dev.local/skin/frontend/default/default/images/btn_checkout.gif`
- `http://magento-dev.local/index.php/checkout/onepage/`
- `http://magento-dev.local/js/varien/accordion.js`
- `http://magento-dev.local/skin/frontend/base/default/js/opcheckout.js`

- ❑ http://magento-dev.local/skin/frontend/default/default/
  images/opc-ajax-loader.gif
- ❑ http://magento-dev.local/skin/frontend/default/default/
  images/cvv.gif
- ❑ http://magento-dev.local/index.php/checkout/onepage/
  progress/?toStep=billing
- ❑ http://magento-dev.local/index.php/electronics/cameras/
  accessories/universal-camera-case
- ❑ http://magento-dev.local/index.php/tag/product/list/
  tagId/185/
- ❑ http://magento-dev.local/index.php/tag/product/list/
  tagId/27/
- ❑ http://magento-dev.local/index.php/customer/account/
  login/

7. You can change the URLs so that they match your Magento configuration. Make sure that the domain matches your configuration and that the URLs exist.

8. Run the following command to start the load test with 50 concurrent users:

```
siege -c50 -i -t 1M -d 3 -f siege_url.txt
```

9. The period for which this script will run depends on the webshop's performance. The output of the command is shown as follows:

```
~$ siege -c50 -i -t 1M -d 3 -f siege_url.txt
** SIEGE 2.70
** Preparing 50 concurrent users for battle.
The server is now under siege...
Lifting the server siege...       done.
Transactions:                2001 hits
Availability:              100.00 %
Elapsed time:               59.48 secs
Data transferred:            0.49 MB
Response time:               0.00 secs
Transaction rate:           33.64 trans/sec
Throughput:                  0.01 MB/sec
Concurrency:                 0.03
Successful transactions:       38
Failed transactions:            0
Longest transaction:         0.04
Shortest transaction:        0.00
```

With the Siege -h command, you can see all the available options.

10. We continue with the configuration of Magento Profiler. To enable the Magento Profiler, open the backend and navigate to **System** | **Configuration** | **Advanced** | **Developer** | **Debug**. Configure the **Profiler** field as shown in the following screenshot:

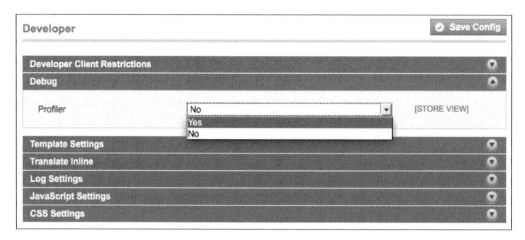

11. To see some more statistics, uncomment the following line in the `index.php` file:

```
Varien_Profiler::enable();
```

12. When you reload the frontend, you will see a grid as shown in the following screenshot:

| Code Profiler | Time | Cnt | Emalloc | RealMem |
|---|---|---|---|---|
| Memory usage: real: 30146560, emalloc: 29423368 | | | | |
| mage | 0.1430 | 1 | 0 | 0 |
| mage::app::init::system_config | 0.0009 | 1 | 141,008 | 0 |
| CORE::create_object_of::Mage_Core_Model_Cache | 0.0020 | 1 | 663,952 | 786,432 |
| mage::app::init::config::load_cache | 0.0033 | 1 | 2,232 | 0 |
| mage::app::init::stores | 0.0164 | 1 | 5,271,376 | 5,242,880 |
| CORE::create_object_of::Mage_Core_Model_Resource_Website | 0.0005 | 1 | 110,208 | 262,144 |
| CORE::create_object_of::Mage_Core_Model_Resource_Website_Collection | 0.0076 | 1 | 2,743,808 | 2,883,584 |
| DISPATCH EVENT:resource_get_tablename | 0.0003 | 34 | 6,096 | 0 |
| CORE::create_object_of::Mage_Core_Model_Resource_Store_Group_Collection | 0.0001 | 1 | 16,168 | 0 |
| CORE::create_object_of::Mage_Core_Model_Resource_Store_Collection | 0.0001 | 1 | 16,136 | 0 |
| mage::app::init_front_controller | 0.0023 | 1 | 540,704 | 524,288 |
| mage::app::init_front_controller::collect_routers | 0.0016 | 1 | 385,136 | 262,144 |
| DISPATCH EVENT:controller_front_init_routers | 0.0005 | 1 | 128,064 | 262,144 |
| OBSERVER: cms | 0.0002 | 1 | 28,936 | 0 |
| mage::dispatch::db_url_rewrite | 0.0020 | 1 | 465,400 | 524,288 |
| mage::dispatch::routers_match | 0.1036 | 1 | 0 | 0 |
| mage::dispatch::controller::action::predispatch | 0.0119 | 1 | 2,922,096 | 2,883,584 |

13. In the previous screenshot, you can see the execution time and memory that is used for each function that is executed. This can help you to find a performance leak.

14. Next, we will install YSlow in Firefox.

    ❑ YSlow is a Firefox plugin that is installed with Firebug

15. To open YSlow, open Firebug by pressing *F12* or by clicking on the icon in the Add-ons bar.

16. After Firebug starts, open the YSlow tab.

17. Check that the **Ruleset** dropdown is set to **YSlow(V2)**.

18. Start the test by clicking on the **Run Test** button.

19. YSlow performs some tests and then displays the results of these tests as shown in the following screenshot:

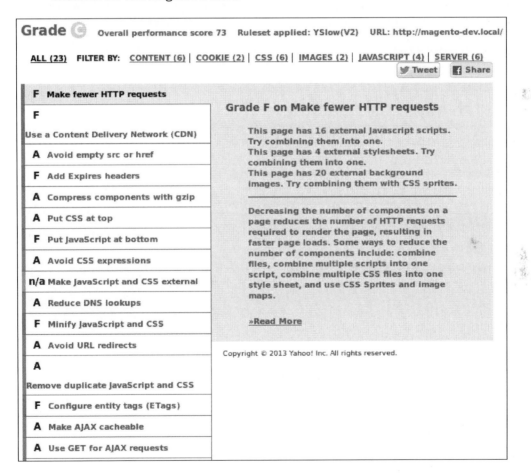

## How it works...

We started with ApacheBench, which is a tool that is installed with the Apache web server. This tool is designed to benchmark the HTTP requests.

We performed a test with a number of concurrent users. When you test with a load of 10 concurrent users, you will simulate a continuous load of 10 requests during the time of the test. When a request is finished, a new one is fired, so there are always 10 processes running.

When you limit the time of the test to 30 seconds, you can see how many successful requests your Apache server has finished during that time. This can give you a good idea of the capacity your web server has.

Siege is a tool similar to ApacheBench. The main difference is that Siege has more options than ApacheBench. In this recipe, we did a load test with a list of URLs. In this list, you can add products to the cart by creating POST requests to simulate a human flow on the webshop. Mostly, product pages are cached but session-specific flows, such as the checkout, can't be cached and will generate more load on your server.

 With ApacheBench and Siege, you can create load on a website. While doing this on a remote website, it is possible that you will be blocked by a firewall because many requests from the same host appear like an attack.

The performance of a web page depends on many factors. YSlow has bundled the most important factors and runs a test with these factors. The parameters are bundled in rulesets. The ruleset we used is the YSlow (V2) that contains most of the checks. You can choose some others or create your own.

When the test runs, YSlow will check all the factors that are in the ruleset. For every factor, it will give a score. The average of all scores is multiplied by the weight of each factor. The weight depends on the impact of every factor on the performance of a website.

In the report generated by YSlow, suggestions are made to get a better score on every specific part. It is up to you to decide which option you will choose to optimize your site.

## There's more...

When your site is on a public URL, you can use some online tools to show a report of your site's performance. These tools will look at your site and generate a report on it. It will make some suggestions just like YSlow does:

▸ **WebPagetest**: This tool can be found at `http://www.webpagetest.org/`
▸ **GTmetrix**: This tool can be found at `http://gtmetrix.com/`

# Optimizing the database and MySQL configuration

When scaling a Magento website, you will have one part that will be a hard job and that is the MySQL database. You can scale your shop with multiple servers but the database is a central storage of all the data of the website, which is not so easy to scale because everything needs to be in sync. In this recipe, we will optimize the Magento MySQL database and the MySQL server.

## Getting ready

Log in to phpMyAdmin and navigate to the next page that shows the information about the database.

## How to do it...

The first step is to optimize the table structures of the Magento database. Take a look at the following procedure:

1.  When you are in phpMyAdmin, click on the Magento database, and you will see the table overview.

2.  At the bottom of this page, click on the **check all** button.

3.  When you click on the drop-down list, you can repair the table and optimize it, as shown in the following screenshot:

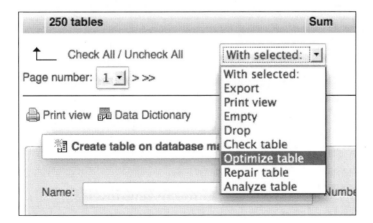

 Make sure you run this action for all the tables in the Magento database. It could happen that the list is separated and presented in multiple pages.

4. When you have repaired and optimized everything, your MySQL database is optimized. You can also replicate the database with the Master/Slave setup as we have done in the *Configuring a Master/Slave setup* recipe in *Chapter 5, Database Concepts*.

The second step is the optimization of the MySQL server. Perform the following steps to optimize the MySQL server:

1. A good server configuration starts with good hardware and the right operating system. To run Magento, it is recommended to use a dedicated server or a VPS. When you use a shared environment, the RAM and CPU load is shared among other users. With a VPS or dedicated server, you have a fixed number of CPUs and a fixed amount of RAM available.

2. When your server is equipped with enough RAM, you can turn off the swapped devices. Sometimes, the swap option will be automatically used even if enough memory is available.

3. In the `my.cnf` file, under the `[mysqld]` section, use the `skip-external-locking` parameter to avoid external locking.

4. The following command is used to set the right value for `key_buffer` in the `MyISAM` tables. To see the configuration, run the following command on the MySQL prompt:

   ```
   mysql> SHOW VARIABLES LIKE '%key_buffer%';
   ```

5. We will set the key buffer size to 512 MB. We can do this by running the following command on the MySQL prompt:

   ```
   mysql> SET GLOBAL key_buffer_size = 536870912;
   ```

6. We will do the following optimization settings in the `my.cnf` file. This is the main configuration file of the MySQL server that is located in the `app/etc/mysql` folder:

   1. Open the file and paste the following configuration under the `[mysqld]` section:

      ```
      [mysqld]
      key_buffer = 512M
      max_allowed_packet = 64M
      thread_stack = 192K
      thread_cache_size = 32
      table_cache = 512
      query_cache_type = 1
      query_cache_size = 52428800
      tmp_table_size = 128M
      expire_logs_days = 10
      max_binlog_size = 100M
      sort_buffer_size = 4M
      ```

```
read_buffer_size = 4M
read_rnd_buffer_size = 2M
myisam_sort_buffer_size = 64M
wait_timeout = 300
max_connections = 400
```

2. Save the file and restart your MySQL server. You can do this by running the following command:

   ```
   sudo service mysql restart
   ```

## How it works...

While optimizing a MySQL server, you have to know the capabilities of your server and the traffic you expect. With these parameters, you can calculate a good value for the key_ buffer, query_cache, and table_cache. Also, think about the skip-external-locking parameter. With this parameter, you can deny external locking.

With the following commands, you can view the MySQL server status:

| Command | More information |
|---|---|
| mysql> SHOW STATUS; | This command shows the current status of the MySQL server. This command is available in MySQL 5.0 and higher, and is the standard to show all the global variables. |
| mysql> SHOW VARIABLES; | All the MySQL variables are shown with this command. |
| mysql> SHOW INNODB STATUS; | This command lets you find out the current INNODB status. |
| mysql> SHOW GLOBAL STATUS; | This command shows the values of the load on the database server for all connections. |
| mysql> SHOW LOCAL STATUS; | This is the same as the SHOW GLOBAL STATUS command, but the values are calculated on the current connection. |
| mysql> mysqladmin extended -i100 -r | Use this command to view what is happening currently with the MySQL server. |

The database optimization is one of the key aspects to tune your Magento webshop. The database optimization amounts to 50 percent of a page load.

# Optimizing the Apache web server

Magento recommends the use of Apache web server when you run a Magento website. There are some other web servers on the market, such as Nginx, but initially Magento was optimized to run on Apache.

The performance of the web server depends mostly on the hardware on which the server is running. Network card, RAM, disk, OS, and CPU are important hardware to think about when you are choosing a server.

## How to do it...

1. The first thing to think about is the OS on which the web server will run. It is highly recommended to use a Linux distribution. In the recipes of this book, we used an Ubuntu server (a Debian-based Linux distribution).

 Don't use a Windows server to run Magento. It will work but it is less efficient and can lead to issues with file permissions, code, and more.

2. Update the OS to the latest stable version because the update software is faster and safer. Use Apache2 instead of the Apache1 series. Apache2 uses fewer CPU resources while delivering static content.

3. Install only the required services on the web server. When a lot of services are installed, you will have background tasks that will use the resources of the server.

4. Use XFS and ReiserFS as the filesystem for a better disk I/O.

5. You have to configure the web server so that it never has to swap. When your web server begins to swap, all requests will be served slower. The first thing is to compare the volume of RAM on the server with the average memory load of a request and the number of requests. The second thing you can do is to configure the `MaxClients` setting. This setting controls the number of child processes when the server swaps.

6. Look at the `HostnameLookups` setting and check if this is configured with the `Off` value.

7. It is not recommended to use the `SymLinksIfOwnerMatch` setting. It is better to use `Options +FollowSymLinks +SymLinksIfOwnerMatch` for specified directories. For other locations, use the `Options +FollowSymLinks` setting to prevent that the system calls `lstat(2)`. The `lstat()` system calls are never cached.

8. Don't use a wildcard syntax in the `DirectoryIndex` setting. The setting is shown as follows:

```
DirectoryIndex index
```

9. It is better to use `index.php` only because Magento uses `index.php` as the default index. This setting is shown as follows:

```
DirectoryIndex index.php
```

10. Enable the `deflate` and `header` Apache modules with the following commands:

**sudo a2enmod deflate**

**sudo a2enmod header**

11. Open the `.htaccess` file in the Magento root and go to the `mod_deflate` configuration tag. Uncomment some lines so that the block looks like the following code:

```
<IfModule mod_deflate.c>

############################################
## enable apache served files compression
## http://developer.yahoo.com/performance/rules.html#gzip

    # Insert filter on all content
    SetOutputFilter DEFLATE
    # Insert filter on selected content types only
    AddOutputFilterByType DEFLATE text/html text/plain text/xml
    text/css text/javascript

    # Netscape 4.x has some problems...
    BrowserMatch ^Mozilla/4 gzip-only-text/html

    # Netscape 4.06-4.08 have some more problems
    BrowserMatch ^Mozilla/4\.0[678] no-gzip

    # MSIE masquerades as Netscape, but it is fine
    BrowserMatch \bMSIE !no-gzip !gzip-only-text/html

    # Don't compress images
    SetEnvIfNoCase Request_URI \.(?:gif|jpe?g|png)$ no-gzip
    dont-vary

    # Make sure proxies don't deliver the wrong content
    Header append Vary User-Agent env=!dont-vary

</IfModule>
```

When you get an internal server error after the change, it is possible that the Apache `headers` module is not enabled. Run the `sudo a2enmod header` command and restart the server to fix this.

12. Take a look at the `KeepAlive` setting of your Apache server. When this is on, the Apache server can serve multiple requests through the same TCP connection.

13. Configure the **MPM (Multi-Processing Modules)** for your case. The values of these configurations depend on the resources and load that you expect on your server.

```
StartServers 50
MinSpareServers 15
MaxSpareServers 30
MaxClients 225
MaxRequestsPerChild 4000
```

14. When you run some load tests again, you can compare the obtained results with the results before the optimization. Usually, you will see some differences.

## How it works...

The performance of a web server depends on many factors. The key parts are the application, the hardware, the OS, and the network.

- ▶ **Application**: The first thing is to ensure that your application is working efficiently with the resources of the server. If your application expects a lot of resources for a request, you can optimize it here.

- ▶ **Hardware**: The second thing is the hardware of the server. You have to make sure that the resources of a server are high enough to serve the expected load and peaks.

- ▶ **OS**: The third thing is the OS and web server. Use a Linux server for Magento with an Apache or Nginx web server on it. Always use the latest version of the software because it is mostly faster and more secured.

- ▶ **Network**: The last thing is the network. The web server sends the response through the network to the client. When that network is slow, the download time of a request will be long. Host your web server with a good network connection and host it in the same region as that of the target audience of your webshop. For example, host your website in Italy for an Italian website.

Optimize the configurations of the system you are using. In this recipe, we did some optimizations to tweak the Apache web server by defining custom settings in the `.htaccess` file.

The last thing is the geographic location of your web server. It is better to locate your web server in the region where your target audience lives. Also, limit the size and number of HTTP requests.

# Tuning the Magento configurations

Magento has some standard features for a better performance, such as caching and compilation. In this recipe, we will configure these features for a better performance of the setup.

## Getting ready

Log in to the admin panel and navigate to the configuration page at **System | Configuration**.

## How to do it...

When you perform the following steps, your Magento installation will run a bit faster:

1. Uninstall or disable the extensions that you are not using.

2. Enable all caching systems that Magento has. They are located at **System | Cache Management**.

 When all caches are enabled, make sure you clear them when you are developing the code.

3. Compile your Magento installation. You can do this by clicking on **Run Compilation Process** on the compilation page at **System | Tools | Compilation**. When the compilation is enabled, all the Magento classes are built in one directory where they will be loaded faster. Compilation can increase the speed by 25 to 50 percent.

4. Disable the unused modules. You can do this by disabling the frontend output by navigating to **System | Configuration | Advanced | Disable Modules Output**. When you're not using the Mage_Poll module, you can disable it here.

5.  Disable some developer features because you don't need them on a live site. Go to **System | Configuration | Advanced | Developers** and configure it as shown in the following screenshot:

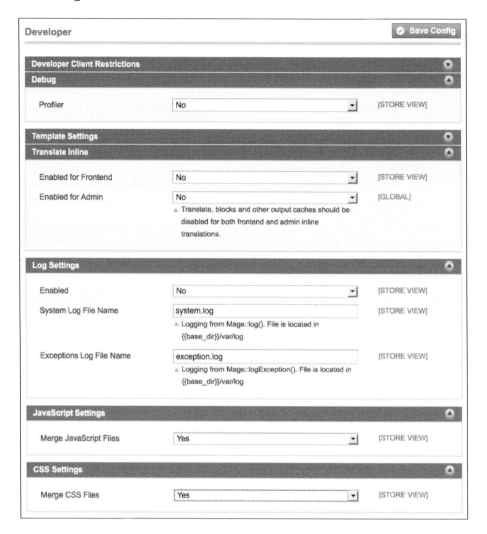

6.  Go to **Catalog | Attributes | Manage Attributes**. When you click on an attribute, you can see the **Frontend Properties** section. Set only those configuration parameters that you want to use in the frontend to **Yes**.

7.  Go to **System** | **Configuration** | **Catalog** and enable the flat catalog product and flat catalog category settings, as shown in the following screenshot. When enabled, a part of the EAV system will be converted to flat tables:

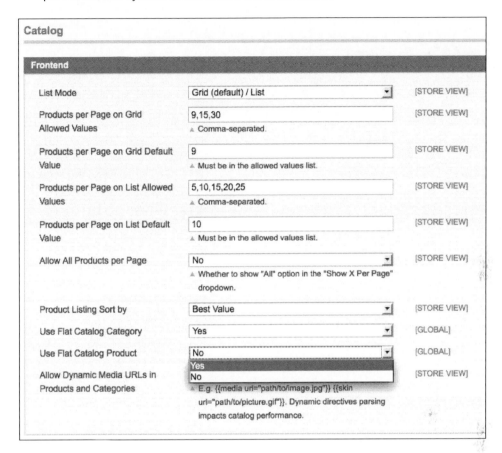

 You can find more information about the flat catalog settings in the *Working with EAV tables* recipe of *Chapter 5, Database Concepts*.

## How it works...

The standard Magento configurations are not the best configurations for an optimal performance. Every option you enable has some impact on the flexibility of development and compatibility with platforms and modules.

When caching is enabled, you will have a better performance. However, you have to keep in mind that you will have to clear it frequently while developing the code, to see your changes in action.

Development features are useful when developing code because it contains interesting information. However, when your site is live, you don't need these features as it will slow down your website. It is recommended that you disable this.

Compilation is a process where Magento will copy all the classes from the `app/code` folder into the `includes` folder. When all the classes are located in one folder, it is faster to load a class instead of looking into all the different module's folders to load a class.

The advantage of compilation is that your site will be faster but a disadvantage is that you have to run the compilation process after every change in the code. When you use a module that doesn't follow the Magento standards, it can lead to errors when compilation is enabled.

The last thing is to enable the flat catalog product and flat catalog category. When you enable these features, Magento will use a flat table for loading products and categories instead of looking in the different EAV tables.

The disadvantages of using this is that you have to sync the data from the EAV tables to the flat tables. When working with a large amount of products and categories, the index process that syncs the data runs for a very long duration.

# Configuring APC and Memcached

The cache system in Magento is based on cache parts of the HTML output and some configuration files. In this recipe, we will configure caching on the PHP level that you can do with APC and Memcached. APC will cache PHP files, while Memcached will cache objects.

## Getting ready

When configuring APC and Memcached for our Magento store, we have to make sure that APC is installed on the server.

To install APC, follow these instructions:

1. On a Debian-based Linux distribution, you can install APC with the following command:

   ```
   sudo apt-get install php-apc
   ```

2. Follow the installer and APC will be available in your PHP configuration.

3. To install Memcached, you can run the following command:

   ```
   sudo apt-get install php5-memcached
   ```

4. To test if the extensions are correctly installed, you can use the `phpinfo()` command. This command gives you a graphical representation of all the available PHP settings.

5. To see `phpinfo`, create a `phpinfo.php` file with the following content:

```
<?php
phpinfo();
```

When you search on APC and Memcached, you will see a block that contains all the settings.

## How to do it...

In the following steps, we will discuss the APC and Memcached configuration in Magento:

1. Make sure APC and Memcached are installed on the server. This is described in the previous section of this recipe.

2. Open the `app/code/local.xml` file and add a `<cache>` block as a child of the `<global>` tag. Your `local.xml` file looks as follows:

```xml
<?xml version="1.0"?>
<config>
 <global>
    <install>
       <date><![CDATA[Mon,
       22 Jul 2013 18:12:54 +0000]]></date>
    </install>
    <crypt>
       <key><![CDATA[cac0174a5563885b926aa73723aeb870]]></key>
    </crypt>
    <disable_local_modules>false</disable_local_modules>
    <resources>
       <db>
         <table_prefix><![CDATA[]]></table_prefix>
       </db>
       <default_setup>
         <connection>
            <host><![CDATA[localhost]]></host>
            <username><![CDATA[root]]></username>
            <password><![CDATA[root]]></password>
            <dbname><![CDATA[magento_dev]]></dbname>
            <initStatements><![CDATA
            [SET NAMES utf8]]></initStatements>
            <model><![CDATA[mysql4]]></model>
```

```
            <type><![CDATA[pdo_mysql]]></type>
            <pdoType><![CDATA[]]></pdoType>
            <active>1</active>
          </connection>
        </default_setup>
      </resources>
      <session_save><![CDATA[files]]></session_save>
      <cache>
        <backend>apc</backend>
      </cache>
    </global>
    <admin>
      <routers>
        <adminhtml>
          <args>
            <frontName><![CDATA[admin]]></frontName>
          </args>
        </adminhtml>
      </routers>
    </admin>
</config>
```

3.  Clear all the Magento caches and restart your Apache server. When you do a load test with ApacheBench, you will see that there is a big improvement in the performance:

```
ab -c 5 -n 100 http://magento-dev.local
```

4.  The previous configuration enables the APC configuration for Magento. With the next configuration, we enable Memcached. We do this by adding a `<cache>` tag as a child of the `<global>` tag. With Memcached, the `local.xml` file will look as follows:

```
<?xml version="1.0"?>
<config>
  <global>
    <install>
      <date><![CDATA[Mon,
      22 Jul 2013 18:12:54 +0000]]></date>
    </install>
    <crypt>
      <key><![CDATA[cac0174a5563885b926aa73723aeb870]]></key>
    </crypt>
    <disable_local_modules>false</disable_local_modules>
    <resources>
      <db>
```

```xml
          <table_prefix><![CDATA[]]></table_prefix>
      </db>
      <default_setup>
        <connection>
          <host><![CDATA[localhost]]></host>
          <username><![CDATA[root]]></username>
          <password><![CDATA[root]]></password>
          <dbname><![CDATA[magento_dev]]></dbname>
          <initStatements><![CDATA
          [SET NAMES utf8]]></initStatements>
          <model><![CDATA[mysql4]]></model>
          <type><![CDATA[pdo_mysql]]></type>
          <pdoType><![CDATA[]]></pdoType>
          <active>1</active>
        </connection>
      </default_setup>
    </resources>
    <session_save><![CDATA[files]]></session_save>
    <cache>
      <backend>memcached</backend>
      <slow_backend>database</slow_backend>
      <memcached>
        <servers>
          <server>
            <host><![CDATA[127.0.0.1]]></host>
            <port><![CDATA[11211]]></port>
            <persistent><![CDATA[1]]></persistent>
            <weight><![CDATA[2]]></weight>
            <timeout><![CDATA[10]]></timeout>
            <retry_interval><![CDATA[10]]></retry_interval>
            <status><![CDATA[1]]></status>
          </server>
        </servers>
        <compression><![CDATA[0]]></compression>
        <cache_dir><![CDATA[]]></cache_dir>
        <hashed_directory_level><![CDATA[]]>
        </hashed_directory_level>
        <hashed_directory_umask><![CDATA[]]>
        </hashed_directory_umask>
        <file_name_prefix><![CDATA[]]></file_name_prefix>
      </memcached>
    </cache>
</global>
```

```
<cache>
  <backend>apc</backend>
</cache>
<admin>
  <routers>
    <adminhtml>
      <args>
        <frontName><![CDATA[admin]]></frontName>
      </args>
    </adminhtml>
  </routers>
</admin>
</config>
```

5. The last thing is to store the `var/cache` folder in memory. We can do this by mounting the folder using TMPFS:

```
mount tmpfs /var/www/packt/magento-dev/var/cache -t tmpfs -o
size=64m
```

## How it works...

**APC** (**Alternative PHP Cache**) is an open source caching framework that optimizes the PHP code, compiles it, and caches it in the shared memory. Executing a precompiled code is faster than loading all the scripts. A common problem with APC is that you have to clear the APC cache before you see any code changes because some parts of the old code are cached.

Memcached is another caching system in PHP. Memcached will cache objects that will be used in the application later. Examples are database objects, sessions, and API calls. Memcached runs on a server, that is, in this example, the same server as the web server. By setting the Magento configuration, we connect to the local Memcached server that runs on port 11211.

In Magento, Memcached increases the performance. In the frontend, there is some effect but the largest effect is in the backend where Magento itself caches very few things.

The last thing was to mount the Magento `cache` folder in the memory. When enough memory is available, it is faster to store the cache files in the RAM memory. When they are located in the RAM, it is faster to load a cache file instead of reading it from the disk.

# Optimizing the PHP configurations

When you are not using an APC such as an accelerator, think about using a PHP accelerator; we will see how in this recipe. When a PHP script is requested, the script will be read and then it will be compiled in binary, which is called opcode. This compiled code will be executed by the PHP engine.

An opcode cache is simply a caching mechanism that saves the compiled code so that the code doesn't have to be compiled every time the script will run. In this recipe, we will optimize the `php.ini` settings for the best performance.

## Getting ready

There are a lot of PHP accelerators on the market, such as APC, eAccelerator, XCache, Zend Accelerator, and Zend Platform. At the following URLs, you can find out more information about these accelerators:

- **APC**: This PHP accelerator can be found at `http://pecl.php.net/package/APC`

- **eAccelerator**: This PHP accelerator can be found at `http://eaccelerator.net/`

- **XCache**: This PHP accelerator can be found at `http://xcache.lighttpd.net/`

## How to do it...

The following steps describe some measures that you can take to improve the PHP configuration:

1. Use an efficient process manager, such as php-fpm, that runs on an impressive speed on FastCGI.

2. Use the `realpath_cache_size` configuration setting to configure the size of the real path cache in PHP. On systems where PHP opens and closes a lot of files, this value needs to be increased. You can use the following setting for Magento:

   ```
   realpath_cache_size=1M
   realpath_cache_ttl=86400
   ```

3. The settings in the following table can improve the performance of the PHP settings:

| Setting | Description | Recommended value |
|---------|-------------|-------------------|
| max_execution_time | This setting sets the maximum time (in seconds) for which a process can live. | 120 |
| max_input_time | This property sets the time (in seconds) for which a script will wait for input data. | 240 |
| memory_limit | With this setting, you can set the amount of memory a process can consume. | For Magento, it is recommended to use 216 MB. |
| output_buffering | With this setting, you can set the amount of bytes to buffer before sending the response to the client. | 4096 |

4. The last thing is to disable some error reporting levels when your site is live. This can be done by using the following setting:

```
error_reporting = E_COMPILE_ERROR|E_ERROR|E_ CORE_ERROR
```

## How it works...

The values in the php.ini configuration depend mostly on the application that you are running and the load that the application will have on your system. If your application has some processes that will run for a long time (this is possible with the re-index process when you have a large number of products), it is required to increase the values of max_execution_time and max_input_time. This is the same for the memory_limit parameter where the recommended value for Magento is 216 MB.

Disabling the error reporting on a production system is recommended for warnings and notices but critical errors need to be reported because this information is required when solving the bug.

# Analyzing the page speed

YSlow is a tool that analyzes the speed for a web page. It is a plugin that you can install in Firebug. While running a report, the site will be tested on some parameters. A report will be shown with an overall score of your website.

The test is based on a ruleset. You have the YSlow (V2) and YSlow (V1) ruleset. We will use the YSlow(V2) ruleset for this recipe, which has 22 rules. The complete page load (including images and static content) can be increased by 25 to 50 percent if you adhere to the following 22 rules:

- ▸ Minimize HTTP requests
- ▸ Use a Content Delivery Network
- ▸ Avoid empty `src` or `href`
- ▸ Add an expires header or a cache-control header
- ▸ Use Gzip for components
- ▸ Put stylesheets at the top
- ▸ Put scripts at the bottom
- ▸ Avoid CSS expressions
- ▸ Make JavaScript and CSS external
- ▸ Reduce DNS lookups
- ▸ Minify JavaScript and CSS
- ▸ Avoid redirects
- ▸ Remove duplicate scripts
- ▸ Configure ETags
- ▸ Make AJAX cacheable
- ▸ Use GET for AJAX requests
- ▸ Reduce the number of DOM elements
- ▸ No 404 errors
- ▸ Reduce the cookie size
- ▸ Use cookie-free domains for components
- ▸ Avoid filters
- ▸ Do not scale images in HTML
- ▸ Make `favicon.ico` small and cacheable

## How to do it...

Perform the following steps to see what we can do with a YSlow result:

1.  Run the YSlow test on the current web page. On a standard Magento webshop, the test normally returns an overall C score.

2.  The first thing is to make fewer HTTP requests. You can fix this by enabling CSS and JS merging. For an optimal score, it is recommended to use sprites so that you have only one background image.

3.  To optimize the background image, you can use an image optimization tool such as Yahoo's Smush.it. When you upload the `images` folder of your theme and run it, you can download the optimized version as shown in the following screenshot:

4.  You can download the optimized images and replace them in the `skin` folder.

5. The next bad point in the test is adding the expires header. We can fix this by modifying some rules in the .htaccess file.

6. The following code shows how to add the expire headers to the static content of the website:

```
<IfModule mod_expires.c>

#############################################
## Add default Expires header
## http://developer.yahoo.com/performance/rules.html#expires

    ExpiresDefault "access plus 1 year"

    ExpiresDefault
    ExpiresActive On
    ExpiresByType image/gif
    ExpiresByType image/jpg
    ExpiresByType image/jpeg
    ExpiresByType image/png
    ExpiresByType image/x-icon
    ExpiresByType text/css
    ExpiresByType application/x-javascript

</IfModule>

#############################################
```

7. With the following code, we will compress some file types:

```
<IfModule mod_deflate.c>

#############################################
## enable apache served files compression
## http://developer.yahoo.com/performance/rules.html#gzip

    # Insert filter on all content
    SetOutputFilter DEFLATE
    # Insert filter on selected content types only
    AddOutputFilterByType DEFLATE text/html text/plain text/xml
    text/css text/javascript

    # Netscape 4.x has some problems...
    BrowserMatch ^Mozilla/4 gzip-only-text/html
```

```
# Netscape 4.06-4.08 have some more problems
BrowserMatch ^Mozilla/4\.0[678] no-gzip

# MSIE masquerades as Netscape, but it is fine
BrowserMatch \bMSIE !no-gzip !gzip-only-text/html

# Don't compress images
SetEnvIfNoCase Request_URI \.(?:gif|jpe?g|png)$ no-gzip
dont-vary

# Make sure proxies don't deliver the wrong content
Header append Vary User-Agent env=!dont-vary

</IfModule>
```

8. The last step is to use a CDN network to host your static images. You can use an existing CDN provider to host the static files of your site, but you can create a subdomain `static.magento-dev.local`, which also points to the Magento root and configures Magento to use this subdomain for static content. You can do this in the backend by navigating to **System | Configuration | General | Web**, as shown in the following screenshot:

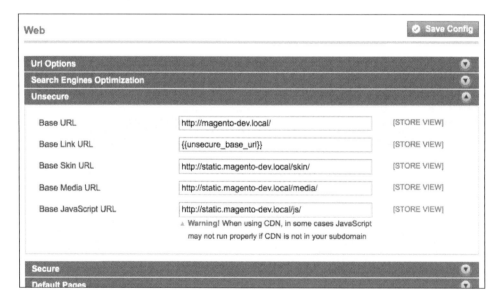

## How it works...

The documentation of all the 22 rules of YSlow is available on their website. If you want more information about a rule, visit the following page that contains all the information:

```
http://developer.yahoo.com/performance/rules.html
```

# 12
# Debugging and Unit Testing

In this chapter, we will cover:

- ▶ Getting started with Xdebug
- ▶ Debugging with FirePHP
- ▶ Installing PHPUnit
- ▶ Creating a Magento test case

## Introduction

Debugging a website in an efficient way is one of the most important jobs of PHP developers. These days, a website is a lot more than some simple HTML pages. In a Magento web shop, you have a lot of complex business logic that is used in the flow of an e-commerce transaction.

Debugging in PHP is not out of the box like in other programming languages. There are many ways to configure a PHP debugger (Xdebug) with a good code editor such as NetBeans. With some extra tools such as FirePHP and the Zend Wildfire plugin, debugging is much easier.

Another part of debugging is automated tests. While working with objects and functions, there are many ways to write some tests that you can run on a set of configured functions. A report will show you the information about the passed and failed tests.

# Getting started with Xdebug

The most common way of debugging a PHP application is to use some functions such as echo, die(), var_dump(), and print_r(). In Magento, you can use the Mage::log() statement to print some logs to a file, but this isn't a real debugger.

With a real debugger, you can break the script and look at the variables and values they have. You can also change values, go further, skip statements, and more.

In PHP, you can configure Xdebug to debug your PHP script or application. In this recipe, we will see how to install Xdebug in the development environment and how we can integrate it with an IDE.

## Getting ready

In this recipe, we will start an Xdebug session with the NetBeans IDE. Open NetBeans and set the **Magento** project as **Main Project**. Make sure all the URLs are configured correctly in the **Property** settings of the project.

## How to do it...

The following steps show you how you can install Xdebug on your development server:

1.  We will install Xdebug with the PHP pear library. Make sure it is installed. If not, run the following commands:

    ```
    sudo apt-get install php5-dev
    sudo apt-get install php-pear
    ```

2.  The next step is to install the xdebug library. You can do this with the following command:

    ```
    sudo pecl install xdebug
    ```

3.  This command gives the following output:

    ```
    Build process completed successfully
    Installing '/usr/lib/php5/20100525/xdebug.so'
    install ok: channel://pecl.php.net/xdebug-2.2.3
    configuration option "php_ini" is not set to php.ini location
    You should add "zend_extension=xdebug.so" to php.ini
    ```

4.  As you can read in the screenshot, we have to locate the xdebug.so file in the php.ini file. To find out the path of the xdebug.so file, run the following command:

    ```
    find / -name 'xdebug.so'
    ```

5. When you have the path, add the following line in the `php.ini` file. Open the file with the following command:

   ```
   sudo nano /etc/php5/apache2/php.ini
   ```

6. Also, do the same for the `cli/php.ini` file:

   ```
   sudo nano /etc/php5/cli/php.ini
   ```

7. Paste the following line of code at the end:

   ```
   zend_extension="/usr/lib/php5/20100525/xdebug.so"
   ```

   Make sure the path matches the path of the `xdebug.so` file on your server.

8. Restart the Apache server with the following command:

   ```
   sudo service apache2 restart
   ```

9. To test if Xdebug is correctly installed, you can check it with `phpinfo()` in the browser or you can run the following command that checks the `phpinfo()` page using the command prompt:

   ```
   php -i | grep xdebug
   ```

10. The previous command gives the following output:

    ```
    xdebug
    xdebug support => enabled
    xdebug.auto_trace => Off => Off
    xdebug.cli_color => 0 => 0
    xdebug.collect_assignments => Off => Off
    xdebug.collect_includes => On => On
    xdebug.collect_params => 0 => 0
    xdebug.collect_return => Off => Off
    xdebug.collect_vars => Off => Off
    xdebug.coverage_enable => On => On
    xdebug.default_enable => On => On
    xdebug.dump.COOKIE => no value => no value
    xdebug.dump.ENV => no value => no value
    xdebug.dump.FILES => no value => no value
    xdebug.dump.GET => no value => no value
    xdebug.dump.POST => no value => no value
    xdebug.dump.REQUEST => no value => no value
    xdebug.dump.SERVER => no value => no value
    xdebug.dump.SESSION => no value => no value
    ```

```
xdebug.dump_globals => On => On

xdebug.dump_once => On => On

xdebug.dump_undefined => Off => Off

xdebug.extended_info => On => On

xdebug.file_link_format => no value => no value

xdebug.idekey => no value => no value

xdebug.max_nesting_level => 100 => 100

xdebug.overload_var_dump => On => On

xdebug.profiler_aggregate => Off => Off

xdebug.profiler_append => Off => Off

xdebug.profiler_enable => Off => Off

xdebug.profiler_enable_trigger => Off => Off

xdebug.profiler_output_dir => /tmp => /tmp

xdebug.profiler_output_name => cachegrind.out.%p => cachegrind.
out.%p

xdebug.remote_autostart => Off => Off

xdebug.remote_connect_back => Off => Off

xdebug.remote_cookie_expire_time => 3600 => 3600

xdebug.remote_enable => Off => Off

xdebug.remote_handler => dbgp => dbgp

xdebug.remote_host => localhost => localhost

xdebug.remote_log => no value => no value

xdebug.remote_mode => req => req

xdebug.remote_port => 9000 => 9000

xdebug.scream => Off => Off

xdebug.show_exception_trace => Off => Off

xdebug.show_local_vars => Off => Off

xdebug.show_mem_delta => Off => Off

xdebug.trace_enable_trigger => Off => Off

xdebug.trace_format => 0 => 0

xdebug.trace_options => 0 => 0

xdebug.trace_output_dir => /tmp => /tmp

xdebug.trace_output_name => trace.%c => trace.%c

xdebug.var_display_max_children => 128 => 128

xdebug.var_display_max_data => 512 => 512

xdebug.var_display_max_depth => 3 => 3
```

11. The next step is to configure the NetBeans Xdebug integration. To make NetBeans work with Xdebug, we have to add the following configuration at the end of the `php.ini` file:

```
xdebug.remote_enable=1
xdebug.remote_handler=dbgp
xdebug.remote_mode=req
xdebug.remote_host=localhost
xdebug.remote_port=9000
xdebug.idekey="netbeans-xdebug"
```

12. Restart your Apache server and look at the `phpinfo()` page to see if the Xdebug settings have been applied.

13. The next step is to check your NetBeans debug settings. Navigate to **Tools | Options** and configure it as shown in the following screenshot:

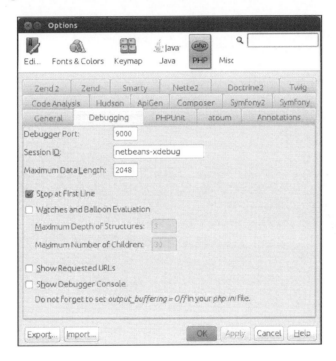

14. The next step is to check if the project URL has the right value. Open the **Project Properties** and go to **Run Configuration**. Make sure the **Project URL** field has the right value as shown the following screenshot:

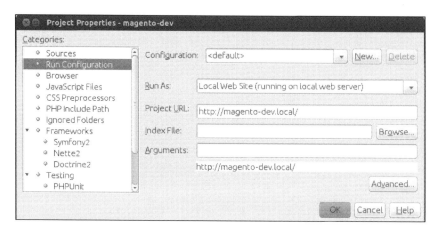

15. We are now ready to start the first debug session. To start it, we have to click on the debug button that is near the run button. You can also use the shortcut *Ctrl + F5*.

16. When starting a debug session, a new tab will be added in the browser with a URL like the following:

```
http://magento-dev.local/?XDEBUG_SESSION_START=netbeans-xdebug
```

17. The web page doesn't load because the debugger is interrupting the process. To continue, we have to use the debugger controls in NetBeans.

18. When you add a breakpoint in the `index.php` file on line 87, `Mage::run($mageRunCode, $mageRunType)`, and continue with the debugger, you will see the variable values as shown in the following screenshot:

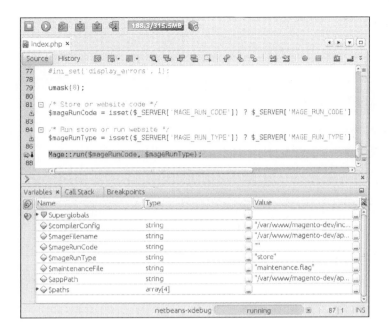

19. When you continue with the breakpoint, you will see that the page will be loaded.

20. The debug session stays alive until you hit the stop button in NetBeans. When you browse to other pages on your website, the debugger will continue as long as the session is alive.

21. To stop the debug session, click on the stop button in NetBeans. A browser page will be opened with the message that the session has stopped.

## How it works...

Xdebug needs to be installed on the server where you want to debug it. In this recipe, the server used is the local debug server.

We installed Xdebug using PEAR. PEAR is an application repository for PHP plugins. With PEAR, we downloaded and installed the xdebug library.

When Xdebug was installed on the server, we configured the php.ini file to use the xdebug library. We added some settings to make the Xdebug configuration compatible with NetBeans.

 When using Xdebug on a remote server, make sure you can connect to the server trough port 9000. This is mostly disabled on the firewall of the server and your local PC.

When the server was configured properly, we checked the configurations in NetBeans and started the debug session. When this session was started, we were able to debug the Magento application like a debugger does it.

The debugger enables advanced debugging features such as the following:

- Setting breakpoints
- Executing the code statement-by-statement
- Skipping parts of code
- Browsing and changing variable names

# Debugging with FirePHP

FirePHP is a plugin that you can install in Firefox. It is integrated in the Firebug console that makes it easy to use as a debugging tool. On the server, FirePHP also needs to be installed. We can do that easily with the PEAR repository, like we did with Xdebug in the previous recipe.

To debug with FirePHP, we need another PHP library. This is the Zend Wildfire plugin in the Zend Framework. Magento is built on the Zend Framework, so the Wildfire plugin is standard installed.

## Getting ready

**FirePHP** is a plugin that runs in **Firebug**. To make them work, we need to install Firebug and FirePHP as Firefox add-ons using the following links:

```
https://addons.mozilla.org/us/firefox/addon/firebug/
```

```
https://addons.mozilla.org/us/firefox/addon/firephp/
```

## How to do it...

The following steps describe how we can use FirePHP in a Magento project:

1. Make sure all the Firefox plugins are installed.
2. Open your Magento project in your IDE such as NetBeans.
3. Open the `index.php` file and add the following code in it at the end of the file:
   ```php
   // --------------------------------------------------------
   // Zend Wildfire log function
   // --------------------------------------------------------
   /**
    * Logs variables to the Firebug Console
    * via HTTP response headers and the FirePHP Firefox Extension.
    *
   ```

```
 * @param mixed $var The variable to log.
 * @param string $label OPTIONAL Label to prepend to the log
   event.
 * @param string $style OPTIONAL Style of the log event.
 * @param array $options OPTIONAL Options to change how messages
   are processed and sent
 * @return boolean Returns TRUE if the variable was added to the
   response headers or buffered.
 * @throws Zend_Wildfire_Exception
 */
function logFirePHP($var, $label = 'Magento vars', $style =
'INFO', $options = array()) {
    if (Mage::getIsDeveloperMode()) {
        $httpRequest = new Zend_Controller_Request_Http();
        $httpResponse = new Zend_Controller_Response_Http();
        $channel = Zend_Wildfire_Channel_
        HttpHeaders::getInstance();
        $channel->setRequest($httpRequest);
        $channel->setResponse($httpResponse);
        ob_start();
        Zend_Wildfire_Plugin_FirePhp::send($var, $label,
        $style, $options);
        $channel->flush();
        $httpResponse->sendHeaders();
    } else {
        return null;
    }
}
// ----------------------------------------------------------
// End Zend Wildfire function
// ----------------------------------------------------------
```

4.  Save the file `index.php`.

5.  Enable the Magento **Profiler** and the Magento developer mode.

6.  We prepared the Magento installation to work with FirePHP. To log something through it, we can use the function `logFirePHP()` to print something in the log. Open the file `app/design/frontend/base/default/template/catalog/product/view.phtml`.

7.  Add the following code at the end of the file:

    ```
    <?php logFirePHP($_product->debug()) ?>
    ```

8. When you open a product detail page and the Firebug console, you should have an output similar to the one shown in the following screenshot:

## How it works...

FirePHP is a logging tool that shows log messages in the Firebug console. We create the log messages with the function `logFirePHP()` that we added in the `index.php` file.

When using the `logFirePHP()` function, a header will be added to the HTTP request. FirePHP will pick up these headers and print them in the Firebug console.

With the function `logFirePHP()`, we can set the log message in the first parameter. This can be any variable such as a string, an array, an object, or something else.

The second parameter is the name of the log message that will show up in the Firebug console.

The last parameter is the type of log message. You can show a message with the following options:

- LOG
- INFO
- WARN
- ERROR
- EXCEPTION
- TRACE
- TABLE
- DUMP
- GROUP_START
- GROUP_END

# Installing PHPUnit

When we want to start with **unit testing** in PHP, we need a tool that is called **PHPUnit**. When PHPUnit is installed, we can start loading tests with the `phpunit` command in the command line.

## Getting ready

Before installing PHPUnit, make sure PEAR is installed on your server. If it is not done, you can do this by running the following command:

```
sudo apt-get install php-pear
```

You can also install it using a file. You can find information about this procedure by navigating to the following URL:

```
http://pear.php.net/manual/en/installation.php
```

## How to do it...

Follow the next steps to install PHPUnit on your development server:

1. To install PHPUnit, we have to use a custom PEAR channel. We need to register the PHPUnit PEAR channel before we can install PHPUnit over PEAR. With the next command, we will add the extra channel to the PEAR environment:

```
sudo pear channel-discover pear.phpunit.de
```

2.  The PHPUnit channel depends on some other channels. We need to discover the channel `components.ez.no` too:

    ```
    sudo pear channel-discover components.ez.no
    ```

3.  The last channel that we have to discover is the **Symfony Components** PEAR channel. With the following command, we will discover the channel `pear.symfony-project.com`:

    ```
    sudo pear channel-discover pear.symfony-project.com

    sudo pear channel-discover pear.symfony.com
    ```

4.  When we have discovered all the required channels, it is time to install the `PHPUnit` library. We can do this by running the following command:

    ```
    sudo pear install phpunit/PHPUnit
    ```

5.  The result of this command will end with the following lines:

    ```
    install ok: channel://pear.phpunit.de/File_Iterator-1.3.4

    install ok: channel://pear.phpunit.de/Text_Template-1.1.4

    install ok: channel://pear.phpunit.de/PHP_Timer-1.0.5

    install ok: channel://pear.phpunit.de/PHP_TokenStream-1.2.1

    install ok: channel://pear.phpunit.de/PHP_CodeCoverage-1.2.13

    install ok: channel://pear.phpunit.de/PHPUnit_MockObject-1.2.3

    install ok: channel://pear.symfony.com/Yaml-2.3.6

    install ok: channel://pear.phpunit.de/PHPUnit-3.7.28
    ```

6.  When running this command, the installer will download and prepare all the required packages so that you can use them.

7.  The last thing is to install the CLI component for PHP. This is most probably installed; if it is not installed, we have to run the following command:

    ```
    sudo apt-get install php5-cli
    ```

8.  The last thing to do is to test that everything we have installed works. To test this, we can run the command `phpunit --version`:

    ```
    $ phpunit -version


    PHPUnit 3.7.28 by Sebastian Bergmann.
    ```

## How it works...

As part of the xUnit, PHPUnit is the most popular framework for PHP unit testing. The xUnit framework contains unit testing frameworks for many programming languages, such as the JUnit for Java.

To install the PHPUnit libraries, we used the PEAR installer (which is an extension of PHP) for downloading and installing extra plugins. To add more plugins, we can add extra channels to PEAR like we did while installing PHPUnit.

## There's more...

When you want to install the PHPUnit library without PEAR, you can do it by using the following steps:

1. The first thing to do is to download the library files that you can find by navigating to the following URL http://pear.phpunit.de/get/.

2. Extract the files in the include_path function that is defined in the php.ini configuration.

3. The next step is to configure the PHPUnit script. First move the phpunit.php file to phpunit.

4. Open the file and replace the string @php_bin@ with your PHP bin path. Usually, this is /usr/bin/php.

5. Copy the file to a location that is in your Linux PATH. Be sure to make the script executable.

6. The last thing to do is to change something in the PHPUnit/Util/PHP.php file. Open this file and change the @php_bin@ string with you PHP bin path. Usually, this is /usr/bin/php.

7. You can now run the phpunit command.

# Creating a Magento test case

For the last recipe of this chapter, we will write an automated test with PHPUnit. PHPUnit is the unit testing framework that we have installed in the previous chapter.

Unit testing is a key part of **Test Driven Development** (**TDD**). With TDD, we will write the test case first, and then we will write the code that returns the expected values that we defined in the test case.

With Magento, which is based on the Zend Framework and built with TDD, it is possible to write unit tests with PHPUnit for a custom or existing module. In this recipe, we will see all the steps that you have to perform for a custom unit test.

## Getting ready

In this recipe, we will create a unit test for the Packt_Helloworld module that we created and extended in *Chapter 4, Creating a Module, Chapter 6, Databases and Modules, Chapter 7, Magento Backend*, and *Chapter 8, Event Handlers and Cronjobs*.

If you don't have the complete code, you can download it from the Packt Publishing website `http://www.packtpub.com`.

## How to do it...

Follow these steps to create a unit test for Magento:

1. Create a folder named `unit-tests` in your Magento root.

2. Create an `autoload.php` file in the `unit-tests` folder.

3. Open the `autoload.php` file and add the following content in it:

```php
<?php

ini_set('include_path', ini_get('include_path') . PATH_SEPARATOR
. dirname(__FILE__) . '/../app' . PATH_SEPARATOR . dirname(__
FILE__));

//Set custom memory limit
ini_set('memory_limit', '512M');

//Include Magento libraries
require_once 'Mage.php';

//Start the Magento application
Mage::app('default');

//Avoid issues "Headers already send"
session_start();
```

4. Create a `phpunit.xml` file in the `unit-tests` folder with the following content:

```xml
<?xml version="1.0" encoding="UTF-8" ?>
<phpunit backupGlobals="false"
        backupStaticAttributes="false"
        colors="true"
        convertErrorsToExceptions="true"
        convertNoticesToExceptions="true"
        convertWarningsToExceptions="true"
        processIsolation="false"
        stopOnFailure="false"
        syntaxCheck="true"
        bootstrap="./autoload.php">
```

```
<testsuite name="Magento Unit Test">
    <directory>./</directory>
</testsuite>
<filter>
    <whitelist>
        <directory>../app/code/local</directory>
    </whitelist>
</filter>
</phpunit>
```

5. The next step is to create a folder tree as shown in the following screenshot:

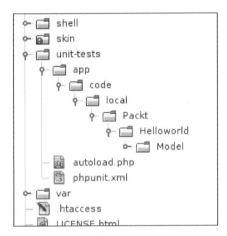

 Instead of creating all the folders manually, you can also run the following Linux command in your terminal: `mkdir -p app/code/local/Packt/Helloworld/Model/`.

6. In the folder `app/code/local/Packt/Helloworld/Model/`, create a new PHP file called `SubscriptionTest.php`.

7. In the `SubscriptionTest.php` file, add the following content:

```php
<?php
class SubscriptionTest extends PHPUnit_Framework_TestCase {

    protected $_subscriptionInstance;

    public function setUp() {
        echo 'Start unit test for method: ' . $this->getName();

        Mage::app('default');
```

```
        $this->_subscriptionInstance = Mage::
        getModel('helloworld/subscription');
    }

    protected function tearDown() {

    }

    public function testGetAllSubscriptions() {
        $subscriptions = $this->_subscriptionInstance-
        >getCollection();

        //Check if $subscriptions is instance of the
        collection class
        $this->assertInstanceOf('Packt_Helloworld_Model_
        Resource_Subscription_Collection', $subscriptions);
    }

}
```

8. To start the unit test, open the terminal and navigate to the `unit-tests` directory of your Magento installation using the following command:

   `cd /var/www/magento-dev/unit-tests`

9. In the `unit-tests` folder, run the `phpunit` command. This will give you an output as shown in the following screenshot:

```
$ phpunit
PHPUnit 3.7.28 by Sebastian Bergmann.

Configuration read from /var/www/magento-dev/unit-tests/phpunit.xml

.Start unit test for method: testGetAllSubscriptions

Time: 94 ms, Memory: 8.75Mb

OK (1 test, 1 assertion)
```

10. When you see the message `OK (1 test, 1 assertion)`, the test has passed.

## How it works...

We started this recipe by creating all the required folders for the unit test. We created the following files:

- ▶ autoload.php
- ▶ phpunit.xml
- ▶ SubscriptionTest.php

The bootstrap of the phpunit command is configured in the phpunit.xml file. In this file, at the beginning of the command, we can configure some parameters that are important. We have configured the loader file autoload.php and some other values of global variables and error-reporting variables.

In the phpunit.xml file, we configured the autoload.php file first in order to run it. In this file, we set the include path with the path of the Magento application, some PHP settings, and the inclusion of the Mage.php file.

The unit test itself is written in the SubscriptionTest.php file. In this file, we created a class that extends the PHPUnit_Framework_Testcase class. This parent class contains all the logic for the unit test and the generic functions.

In the setup() function, we can write some code to bootstrap the test. In this case, we created an instance of the subscriptions collection.

The unit test is in the testGetAllSubscriptions() method. The phpunit command will run all the test* functions in that class. In this function, we used the function assertInstanceOf() to see if the type of the class matches the value that is set in the first parameter.

## There's more...

In this case, we used the assertion function assertInstanceOf() that will look at the instance type of the variable. There are many more assertion functions that you can use with PHPUnit. For example, a function that compares a number and a function to check for null values.

A full list of the assertion methods can be found at the following URL:

http://phpunit.de/manual/3.7/en/writing-tests-for-phpunit.
html#writing-tests-for-phpunit.assertions

# Index

## V

value key  144
Varien_Data_Collection class  116
Varien_Data_Collection_Db class  117
Varien_Object class  154
version control
  adding, to source code  15-18

## W

WAMP (Windows, Apache, MySQL, and PHP)
    10
WebPagetest tool
  about  206
  URL  212
website limits
  exploring, steps  205-212
  exploring, tools  204
widget configuration file
  creating  183, 184
  initializing  182
  testing  183
  working  185
Widget Options tab  42, 184
widgets
  about  40
  adding, to layout  40-42
widget theming
  finalizing  198-201
Wiz
  URL  22

wiz admin-createadmin command  22
wiz admin-resetpass command  22
wiz cache-clear command  22
wiz devel-showhints command  22
wiz module-list command  22
wiz sql-cli command  22
WYSIWYG editor  59

## X

XCache  227
Xdebug
  advanced debugging features  240
  installation, testing  235-239
  installing, on development server  234, 235
  working  239

## Y

YouTube video
  embedding  58, 59
YSlow result
  experimenting  230-232
YSlow tool
  about  206
  opening  211

## Z

Zend_Log class  148

## Thank you for buying
# Magento 1.8 Development Cookbook

# About Packt Publishing

Packt, pronounced 'packed', published its first book "*Mastering phpMyAdmin for Effective MySQL Management*" in April 2004 and subsequently continued to specialize in publishing highly focused books on specific technologies and solutions.

Our books and publications share the experiences of your fellow IT professionals in adapting and customizing today's systems, applications, and frameworks. Our solution based books give you the knowledge and power to customize the software and technologies you're using to get the job done. Packt books are more specific and less general than the IT books you have seen in the past. Our unique business model allows us to bring you more focused information, giving you more of what you need to know, and less of what you don't.

Packt is a modern, yet unique publishing company, which focuses on producing quality, cutting-edge books for communities of developers, administrators, and newbies alike. For more information, please visit our website: www.packtpub.com.

# About Packt Open Source

In 2010, Packt launched two new brands, Packt Open Source and Packt Enterprise, in order to continue its focus on specialization. This book is part of the Packt Open Source brand, home to books published on software built around Open Source licences, and offering information to anybody from advanced developers to budding web designers. The Open Source brand also runs Packt's Open Source Royalty Scheme, by which Packt gives a royalty to each Open Source project about whose software a book is sold.

# Writing for Packt

We welcome all inquiries from people who are interested in authoring. Book proposals should be sent to author@packtpub.com. If your book idea is still at an early stage and you would like to discuss it first before writing a formal book proposal, contact us; one of our commissioning editors will get in touch with you.

We're not just looking for published authors; if you have strong technical skills but no writing experience, our experienced editors can help you develop a writing career, or simply get some additional reward for your expertise.

## Magento 1.4 Development Cookbook

ISBN: 978-1-84951-144-5        Paperback: 268 pages

Extend your Magento store to the optimum level by developing modules and widgets

1. Develop Modules and Extensions for Magento 1.4 using PHP with ease

2. Socialize your store by writing custom modules and widgets to drive in more customers

3. Achieve a tremendous performance boost by applying powerful techniques such as YSlow, PageSpeed, and Siege

## Magento Beginner's Guide
### *Second Edition*

ISBN: 978-1-78216-270-4        Paperback: 320 pages

Learn how to create a fully featured, attractive online store with the most powerful open source solution for e-commerce

1. Install, configure, and manage your own e-commerce store

2. Extend and customize your store to reflect your brand and personality

3. Handle tax, shipping, and custom orders

Please check **www.PacktPub.com** for information on our titles

## Magento PHP Developer's Guide

ISBN: 978-1-78216-306-0     Paperback: 256 pages

Get started with the flexible and powerful e-commerce framework, Magento

1. Build your first Magento extension, step by step

2. Extend core Magento functionality, such as the API

3. Learn how to test your Magento code

## Mastering Magento

ISBN: 978-1-84951-694-5     Paperback: 300 pages

Maximize the power of Magento: for developers, designers, and store owners

1. Learn how to customize your Magento store for maximum performance

2. Exploit little known techniques for extending and tuning your Magento installation

3. Step-by-step guides for making your store run faster, better and more productively

Please check **www.PacktPub.com** for information on our titles

Printed in Great Britain
by Amazon.co.uk, Ltd.,
Marston Gate.